# JOSEPH, MARY, JESUS

Lucien Deiss, C.S.Sp.

Translated by
Madeleine Beaumont

*A Liturgical Press Book*

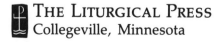
THE LITURGICAL PRESS
Collegeville, Minnesota

Cover design by Ann Blattner. "Christ Discovered in the Temple" by Simone Martini. Walker Art Gallery, Liverpool, Great Britain. Used with permission, Bridgeman/Art Resource, NY.

1    2    3    4    5    6    7    8    9

**Library of Congress Cataloging-in-Publication Data**

Deiss, Lucien.
   [Joseph, Marie, Jésus.  English]
   Joseph, Mary, Jesus / Lucien Deiss ; translated by Madeleine Beaumont.
     p.   cm.
   Translated from an original French manuscript.
   Includes bibliographical references and index.
   ISBN 0-8146-2255-0
   1. Jesus Christ—Childhood.  2. Jesus Christ—Family.  3. Jesus Christ—
Biography.  I. Title.
BT320.D4513  1996
232.92—dc20                                    95-31716
                                                               CIP

# Contents

# JOSEPH, MARY,
# JESUS

# Introduction

Today, we say, "Jesus, Mary, and Joseph." In the past, in Nazareth, they said, "Joseph, Mary, and Jesus." Or else, in a more informal way, "Joseph, Mary, and the little one." The object of this essay is to reflect on Jesus' childhood, when he was learning to become a full grown man.

Of course, the mystery remains, the mystery of the incarnation, the mystery of the One whom our Creed acclaims as "Light from light, true God from true God" and who became a human being. But it is in the subdued light of Nazareth that this mystery shines most brilliantly, to the point of dazzling the eyes of our hearts.

He dominates the eternal ages, but Joseph and Mary gazed on him as a newborn lying in a manger. Teacher of wisdom, new Moses, he proclaimed the new law of his gospel, "You have heard that it was said. . . . But I say to you. . . ." But Joseph and Mary were the ones who taught him to speak, with this Galilean accent which was so easily detected in Jerusalem.[1] Eternal Word, maker of the universe, he holds the stars in his hand[2] and leads the dance of the countless galaxies. But Joseph taught him how to plane a board and use a T square. He is the Lord of majesty who at the end of time will sit on his throne of glory,[3] surrounded by all his holy angels. But his first throne was his mother's lap where he only had to turn his head to reach the source of milk.

---

1. Matt 26:73.
2. Rev 1:16.
3. Matt 25:31.

What are the "sources" of Jesus' formation? We may think first of the tradition of Israel, then of the family traditions of Joseph and Mary, and finally of what Jesus discovered on his own in his relation with God.

*Son of Israel,* Jesus inherited the rich tradition of the people of the Covenant. From this angle, his formation was similar to that received by boys and girls in the Nazareth of his time, even if we admit that in his case it was a special success. Obviously, this tradition comprised, first of all, written revelation, that is, what we call the Old Testament, but also the orally transmitted laws which were in use in Jesus' time and were collected in the Mishnah.[4] To know this tradition is to have access to the surroundings in which Jesus' formation took place.

*Son of Mary and Joseph,* who by reason of their vocation had entered into an intimate friendship with God, Jesus grew up at the heart of this friendship. Of course, we do not know how Joseph and Mary, in their home, in God's presence, lived the love that united them, and we can only imagine their hands joined in a gesture of mutual tenderness and offering to God. But Jesus' perfect balance both on the human and religious planes reveals the quality of the love which united Joseph and Mary.

*Son of God,* among God's sons and daughters journeying with him to the Father, Jesus strengthened day by day this filial and personal relationship which united him to the Father in heaven—first in the play of his childhood, then in the exhilaration of his adolescence, in the work of his adult years, and finally in his messianic ministry, including his death. This relationship remained his most secret garden, in some way the paradise in which his soul lived. His prayers remain for us an abyss of silence. Those which are recorded in the Gospels are like flashes of light revealing the sun that shone in his heart. His ultimate entreaty on the cross, when he had entered the absolute solitude before God, when all his paths were engulfed in darkness, expresses a total abandonment to the Father: "Father, into your hands I commend my spirit."[5] This prayer was

---

4. It is believed that the redactional work which resulted in the Mishnah began about the end of the second century B.C.E. and was completed by Rabbi Yehuda ha-Nasi (135–217) who gave it its definitive form. See H. L. Strack and G. Stemberger, *Introduction au Talmud et au Midrash* (Paris: Cerf, 1986) 141–84.

5. Luke 23:46.

the conclusion of his life as son of God, begun in Nazareth between Joseph and Mary.

This work was written with joy and wonder. One also felt the burden of modesty and humility. For example, even though we are conversant with the laws and customs set down in the Mishnah, we do not know to what extent Joseph and Mary accepted to submit to each of its prescriptions. Also, how can we evaluate Jesus' psychological and spiritual evolution? To evaluate this for any human being is difficult; Jesus' remains a pure mystery.[6] Some of our assertions have the fragility of hypotheses. However, a hypothesis may claim credibility insofar as it appears reasonable. Thus, nowhere is it said that the couple Joseph and Mary—a couple willed and ratified by God[7]—lived in harmony, that they walked hand in hand toward the reign. Nevertheless, we can reasonably grant this. Similarly, we can also grant a second one, that their prefect accord exerted a considerable influence on Jesus' human formation.

The splendor of his humanity reveals as in a mirror the beauty of Joseph's and Mary's humanity.

✢

Although rooted as deeply as possible in the Word of God, this essay is not simply an exegetical study. Rather, what we have here is a wonder-filled gazing, in the light of Scripture and Tradition, upon the most sublime reality that God has created on earth, that is, the love between a man and a woman—here Joseph and Mary—a love whose single focus was their love for their child, Jesus.

In order to be able to contemplate and understand spiritual realities, the Pauline tradition states that the Father of glory must enlighten "the eyes of [the] heart" (Eph 1:18). It is with these eyes, illuminated by the Spirit, that it is fitting to admire God's marvels.

Lucien Deiss, C.S.Sp.
Pentecost 1994

6. P. Grelot writes, "Only with extreme discretion can we approach the psychological and spiritual evolution of the adolescent Jesus whom the evangelists have left in quasi-obscurity." See "Joseph (Saint)" in *Dictionnaire de Spiritualité,* 16 vols. (Paris: Beauchesne, 1932–1994) 8:1296. We remain on the strictly scriptural plane here. For a theological study of Jesus' consciousness, see for instance B. Lauret, *Initiation à la Pratique de la Théologie Dogmatique,* vol. 1 (Paris: Cerf, 1982) 335–39.

7. Matt 1:20.

# Chapter 1
# Joseph and Jesus

## JOSEPH THE FATHER OF JESUS

### Joseph's Fatherhood

In John's Gospel, Joseph is presented as Jesus' father without any further specification. Thus Philip, after his initial meeting with Jesus, says to Nathanael, "We have found him about whom Moses in the law and also the prophets wrote, *Jesus son of Joseph* from Nazareth." And in the synagogue of Capernaum during his discourse on the bread of life, when Jesus declares that he is coming from heaven, the Jews murmur among themselves, "Is not this Jesus, the son of Joseph, whose father and mother we know?"[1]

Luke's Gospel uses the same vocabulary. About the presentation of the little child in the Temple, Luke writes, *"The child's father and mother* were amazed at what was being said about him." And later on, at the finding in the Temple, when Jesus is twelve years old, Mary says to him, "Child, why have you treated us like this? Look, *your father and I* have been searching for you in great anxiety."[2]

Now, according to the traditions of both Matthew and Luke,[3] Joseph had no part in Jesus' conception. Only "the Holy Spirit" and

1. John 1:45; 6:42.
2. Luke 2:33, 48.
3. Matt 1:20; Luke 1:35.

"the power of the Most High" had been at work. Moreover, when Luke relates Jesus' genealogy, he notes that Jesus "was the son (as was thought) [*hōs enomizeto*] of Joseph."[4] Then, how can Joseph be called Jesus' father?

We commonly say, when we are content with a general affirmation, that Joseph can be called Jesus' father, as he is in Scripture, simply because Jesus was born of Mary, Joseph's spouse. Indeed, there was a real marriage between Joseph and Mary when, on the angel's advice, he took her into his home even though she was pregnant. And there was full and public recognition of fatherhood when, again on the angel's advice, Joseph named the infant: "you are to name him Jesus."[5] Joseph's claim to fatherhood is therefore based on his marriage to Mary, the child's mother.

We can add that according to biblical tradition, fatherhood is always a call from God to welcome the child as a gift of God's love. Ever since the Covenant with Abraham, of which the external sign is circumcision, fertility has been the blessing par excellence which God grants to those who love God.[6] More than any other fatherhood, Joseph's was a call from the God of the Covenant to welcome into his family this heaven-sent child.

Is there a title to designate such fatherhood? Several have been proposed, all rather colorless. Supposed father? But Joseph and Mary's union is not a supposed, but a real marriage. Adoptive father? But one does not adopt one's own child. Foster father? But all fathers must feed their children. Spiritual father? But all fathers must "raise" their children, according to the most elevated meaning of the word "raise." Truly, there is no title on earth to designate such a fatherhood. The mystery of this fatherhood is akin to that of Mary's motherhood. Never in the history of humankind was there ever a virginal motherhood, a motherhood like Mary's. And never was there a fatherhood like Joseph's. When we say "virginal motherhood," we do not explain the mystery; we simply give it a name, the name befitting it according to the Scriptures. For it would not have been any more difficult for divine omnipotence to become incarnate in a human egg naturally fertilized in an ordinary conju-

---

4. Luke 3:23. One should note that the traditions of Matthew and Mark seem independent from each other.

5. Matt 1:20-21.

6. Ps 128:3-4.

gal union than in an egg not humanly fertilized.[7] When we speak of Joseph's fatherhood, neither do we explain the mystery; we simply give it a name, the name we read in the Scriptures. What gives this fatherhood its inexpressible beauty remains a secret between God and Joseph.

### "The Child Grew and Became Strong"

Twice, Luke takes note of the human progress in Jesus' growth. He concludes the episode of the presentation in the Temple by saying:

> The child grew and became strong, filled with wisdom; and the favor of God was upon him.[8]

And after the finding of Jesus in the Temple among the teachers, he says:

> And Jesus increased in wisdom and in years, and in divine and human favor.[9]

We easily understand that Jesus was growing in size. He was like all newborns, and like all babies, progressively identified himself with his body, sucked his thumb, tried to grasp his big toe. Having become a toddler, he began to ask those naive and guileless questions which are the earmark of childhood and which brought smiles to Joseph's and Mary's faces. Then he became a teenager. He underwent the crisis of puberty and did not fail to notice, among the neighborhood girls, some Rebekah or Judith who seemed to be interested in him. Then he became an adult. The Romans used to say, *Filii matrizant*, "Sons resemble their mothers." As he grew up, Jesus resembled his mother more and more. We easily understand the process of growing up: it is part of the journey of every human being "born of woman," as Scripture says.

---

7. J. Ratzinger declares, "According to the faith of the Church, Jesus' divine filiation does not rest on the fact that Jesus did not have a human father. The teaching concerning Jesus' divinity would not be affected *(würde nicht angetastet)* if Jesus had been born from a normal human marriage. *Einführung in das Christentum*, 5th ed. München: Kosel, 1968) 225, quoted in R. Pesch, *Das Markusevangelium*, Herders Kommentar 1 (1976) 323.

8. Luke 2:40.

9. Luke 2:52.

Luke also states that Jesus "increased in wisdom." He progressively discovered his father and mother, recognized the sound of their voices and the features of their faces. He learned his first Aramaic words: *imma* ("mama") and *abba* ("daddy"). On the day when, for the first time, he said *abba*, Joseph felt his heart melt with tenderness. And to this child, both so mysterious and so close, born of the Holy Spirit, he whispered this marvelous word, *tinoki* ("my little one"). Later on, when Jesus pronounced words at which heaven and earth were shaken, he pronounced them in the tone of Joseph's voice. And when he smiled upon the children and the poor, his lips reproduced the smile of Mary, his mother.

Jesus learned very early to read and write. About the first century of our era, it was generally advised that at the age of five a child begin the study of Scripture; at ten, that of the Mishnah; at thirteen (the age at which boys were supposed to have reached puberty, whereas girls had done so one year earlier), the practice of the commandments; at fifteen, the study of the Talmud.[10]

The teaching of boys was an obligation rightfully incumbent on the father.[11] Joseph, the righteous man, surely did not shirk this duty. And like all loving wives, Mary surely helped him in this task.

## The Languages Jesus Spoke

### Aramaic

Jesus' mother tongue was Aramaic. It surfaces in the Greek texts of the Gospels, especially in Mark's. Thus, we learn that Jesus gave James and John the name *Boanerges*, that is, "Sons of Thunder."[12] At the raising of Jairus' daughter, we hear Jesus say to the child *talitha koum*, which is the Greek transcription of the Aramaic *talita qumi* ("little girl, get up"). We see Jesus touch the ears and tongue of the deaf man who had an impediment in his speech; we hear him sigh and say *Ephphatha*,[13] which is the Greek transcription of the Aramaic *etpatah* ("be opened").[14] Mark is also the only one to give

10. Strack-Billerbeck, 2:146.
11. Ch. Rabin, "Hebrew and Aramaic in the First Century," Safrai-Stern, 1034.
12. Mark 3:17.
13. *Talitha koum*, Mark 5:41; *Ephphatha*, Mark 7:34.
14. Mark 7:34.

us the invocation, full of filial tenderness, of the prayer in Gethsemane, "Abba, Father," which Matthew is content with transcribing into the Greek "my Father."[15] We are deeply distressed by the heart-rending cry on Golgotha, *Eloi, Eloi, lema sabachthani*,[16] which is the Aramaic translation of the Hebrew of Psalm 22:2, "My God, my God, why have you forsaken me?"

Aramaic is attested as early as the ninth century B.C.E. in northern Syria. The modern Western Aramaic is still spoken today in three Syrian Christian villages of the Anti-Lebanon: Maaloula, Bakha, and Djoubadim. The Aramaic which Jesus spoke was what is called Middle Aramaic (spoken from the second century B.C.E. until the third century C.E.). It comprised numerous dialects which corresponded to several easily discernible geographic areas. Each area also had its own particular accent which people of the time were well acquainted with. During the painful scene of Peter's denial when a servant-girl stares at him and says, "You also were with Jesus, the man from Nazareth," it is enough for Peter to answer with a single sentence, "I do not know or understand what you are talking about," to be recognized and assailed, "Certainly you are also one of them; for you are a Galilean" and "your accent betrays you."[17] Peter's accent was that of the region around the Lake of Galilee: Peter was a native of Bethsaida and lived with his mother-in-law in Capernaum by the lake.[18] This accent must have resembled Jesus': Nazareth is located about thirty kilometers from Capernaum as the crow flies.

People have long recognized the widespread fact of *diglossia*[19]: besides the more or less official language of written texts and religious documents, any linguistic community ordinarily uses a simplified manner of speech for everyday conversation. The dialect Jesus

15. Mark 14:36; Matt 26:39.
16. Mark 15:34.
17. Mark 14:66-70; Matt 26:73.
18. According to John 1:44, Bethsaida is the city of Andrew and Peter. According to Mark 1:29, Jesus comes to the house of Peter and Andrew in Capernaum and heals Peter's mother-in-law.
19. *Diglossia*, from *dis* ("twice") and *glossa* ("language"). On *Diglossia*, see Rabin, "Hebrew and Aramaic," 1008. *Diglossia* is found in all languages having a written literature, for instance, in French, where there is a difference between the written text and certain patois; in German, where there is a difference between *Hoch-Deutsch* and Platt-deutsch; in Arabic, where there is a difference between literary Arabic and everyday language.

spoke was not the polished literary Aramaic one meets in Targumic literature or in the Aramaic passages of Ezra or Daniel or in the Qumran texts, but the popular Aramaic spoken on the streets. When Jesus spoke of the Pharisees as camel-swallowers and gnat-strainers,[20] he must have used an unvarnished language everyone understood.

However, despite its popular character, Jesus' speech was sometimes invested with an unparalleled power. When the chief priests and Pharisees sent Temple police to arrest him, they came back empty-handed with this excuse, "Never has anyone spoken like this."[21] In fact, in the texts where the Greek translation has not destroyed the original Aramaic, the emotion of prophetic utterance is still perceptible. Here is a literal reconstruction of the conclusion of the Sermon on the Mount:

> Whoever listens to these words of mine
> and practices them
> will be like a well-advised person
> who built his or her house on the rock.
> And fell the downpour,
> and came the torrents,
> and blew the tornadoes,
> and they were unleashed against this house.
> But it did not collapse!
> For it had been built on the rock.[22]

From whom did Jesus get this gift of prophetic speech since it was public knowledge that he had not gone to any school?[23] From the Holy Spirit, some will say. Undoubtedly. But the Spirit had similarly inspired the ancient prophets, yet all had kept their own personalities, their good qualities as well as defects. Without question, Jesus received this gift from his surroundings. Now, this environment was first of all the familial community of Joseph and Mary.

### Hebrew

It was in his family environment that Jesus very early became proficient in *Hebrew*, regarded as a sacred language. Tradition

20. Matt 23:24.
21. John 7:46.
22. Matt 7:24-25.
23. John 7:15.

taught: "It was said, 'When young children begin to talk, their fathers must speak to them in the holy language and teach them the Law. Not to speak to them in the holy language and not to teach them the Law is tantamount to letting them die.' "[24] Again, we have good reason to think Joseph was not remiss in giving Hebrew lessons to his child.

Jesus was in perfect command of Hebrew and handled the scrolls of the Law with great familiarity. This is evident from his reading in the Nazareth synagogue. Luke recounts: "He went to the synagogue on the sabbath day, as was his custom. He stood up to read."[25] The *hazzan* ("attendant" of the synagogue) handed him the scroll of the prophet Isaiah. Having "unrolled the scroll, he found the place where it was written:

> The Spirit of the Lord is upon me,
> because he has anointed me
>     to bring good news to the poor."[26]

The scrolls of Scripture were rolled beginning with the end. Thus, the beginning of the scroll contained the beginning of Isaiah. In order to reach the sixty-first chapter, where the text read by Jesus was written, he had to unroll over five meters of scroll. Furthermore, in spite of its division into paragraphs to make the reading easier,[27] the Hebrew text was continuous without headings and without vowels (the text contained only consonants). Therefore, Jesus had an intimate knowledge not only of Hebrew but also of the Book of Isaiah, and particularly Deutero-Isaiah from which the text read at Nazareth was taken. On the basis of references and allusions found in the New Testament, some have stated that Deutero-Isaiah was "Jesus' favorite book."[28] In all likelihood, Jesus must have inherited this predilection for Deutero-Isaiah from Joseph and Mary.

It is legitimate to suppose that Jesus' prayer moved freely throughout the Psalter. It was "the book of songs and prayers of

---

24. Sifre Deut 46, quoted by Rabin, "Hebrew and Aramaic," 1034.

25. Luke 4:16.

26. Luke 4:17-18. "Having unrolled" *(anaptuxas)*. There is another version, less well attested, "having opened" *(anoixas)*.

27. See Ch. Perrot, "Les alinéas dans les rouleaux prophétiques," *La lecture de la Bible dans la Synagogue* (Hildesheim: Gerstenberg, 1973) 108-13.

28. P.-E. Bonnard, *Le Second-Isaïe*, Etudes Bibliques (Paris: Gabalda, 1972) 81.

the post-exilic community."[29] Matthew and Mark mention the hymn singing *(humnēsantes)*, that is, the Hallel, at the Last Supper.[30] The Hallel comprises Psalms 113 to 118, called the "little Hallel," and Psalm 136, called the "great Hallel." Jesus and his disciples probably sang the Hallel by heart. Now, Passover, even though celebrated in Jerusalem, remained a family feast. It was with Joseph and Mary that the child Jesus learned to sing and committed to memory the Psalms of the Hallel. The refrain of Psalm 118, repeated in Psalm 136, the great Hallel,

> O give thanks to the LORD, for he is good;
> his steadfast love endures forever![31]

supported his paschal joy. Learned at Joseph's and Mary's knees, this refrain, which acclaims God's eternal love, would accompany him all his life. It was his last song with his disciples. And when they all had abandoned him, when he was alone before death, this refrain was the cry of his faith in the Father's love.

## Greek

Did Jesus know Greek? Probably a little, like many Jews of his time.[32]

He talked with the centurion of Capernaum, whose servant he was about to heal; with the Canaanite woman who "was a Gentile, of Syrophoenician origin" (which means that she was a pagan and probably spoke Greek[33]), whose daughter he was about to heal; probably with the Greeks who had said to Philip, "We wish to see Jesus"; with Pilate when he was brought to his headquarters.[34] Nothing suggests the presence of an interpreter in these conversations.

The Greek Jesus spoke was that of *common* speech, whence the name Koine, *common* language. The period of Alexander the Great (d. 323 B.C.E.) is usually regarded as marking the end of Attic Greek

29. H.-J. Kraus, *Psalmen*, Biblischer Kommentar, Altes Testament (Neukirchen: Neukirchener Verlag, 1960) xviii.

30. Matt 26:30; Mark 14:26.

31. Pss 118:1, 29; 136:1 (see also v. 26).

32. See G. Mussies, "Greek in Palestine and the Diaspora," Safrai-Stern, 1040–1064; M. Carrez, *Les langues de la Bible* (Paris: Centurion, 1983) 83–88.

33. Pesch, *Markusevangelium*, 1:390.

34. References: Matt 8:6-13; Mark 7:26-29; 18:33-38; John 12:20-21; 19:8-11.

(customarily considered the model of classical Greek) and the start of the spreading of Koine. This spreading was considerably accelerated by Alexander's conquests. Yesterday, as today, the rule was that the victor's language became the language of the vanquished and occupied territories. In Jesus' time, Koine had become the usual means of communication throughout the Mediterranean world.

Moreover, we must remember that Palestine, much before the ruin of Jerusalem and the deportation to Babylon in 587 B.C.E., therefore much before Alexander the Great, was open to multiple linguistic influences. Galilee in particular, being at the crossroads of the routes linking Egypt to the Fertile Crescent, fully deserved its name *Gelil haggoyim* ("the region of the nations").[35] We find Jewish inscriptions written in Greek even in synagogues, especially in Galilee.[36]

Koine Greek was often written, therefore pronounced, in an imprecise way.[37] And it is not evident that those who spoke it—including Jesus—knew how to write or read it. But it was the means of communication, not only between the Jews of the Diaspora and the "nations," but also among the Jews of the Diaspora themselves. At the time of the first Christian Pentecost, Luke writes, "devout Jews from all nations under heaven"[38] were in Jerusalem. They were able to communicate among themselves thanks to Koine. It was precisely for such people speaking multiple languages that the evangelists and their circles wrote the Gospels, not in the ancient sacred language, Hebrew, but in everyday language, Koine. Jesus must have had some knowledge of Koine.

---

35. Isa 8:23, quoted in Matt 4:15.
36. Carrez, *Les langues*, 87.
37. Mussies, "Greek in Palestine," 1042, speaks of the transformation of the diphthongs *ai* into *e*, *oi* into *u*, and *ei* into *i*. *Keitai* ("here lies") becomes simply *kite* (p. 1043). The phenomenon of iotacism—which is a general phenomenon—is naturally found in Jewish inscriptions.
38. Acts 2:5.

## JOSEPH THE CARPENTER

People said of Jesus, "Is not this the carpenter's son?" or "Is not this the carpenter, the son of Mary?"[1] Joseph was a carpenter and Jesus followed in his father's footsteps. Fathers who taught their sons the crafts they themselves plied were the objects of praise.[2] About the middle of the second century, Christian circles still kept the memory of the yokes and plows Jesus had made. In his *Dialogue with Trypho the Jew*, a work dating back to about 150, Justin writes: "When Jesus came to the Jordan [to be baptized], he was believed to be the son of Joseph the carpenter. . . . He was believed to be himself a carpenter because during the time he spent among human beings, he was engaged in carpentry work: plows and yokes."[3]

The carpenter's trade *(tektōn)* was held in high esteem.[4] For example, among the Talmudic adages concerning a matter difficult to explain or understand, it is said, "This is a thing not even a carpenter, son of carpenter—it being implied 'as educated as he might be'—can explain."[5] We should probably not try to specify too narrowly what the term "carpenter" meant and think of it as designating an artisan working with wood in general and not just a framer. Only princely dwellings and the mansions of rich people had roofs supported by wooden joists; ordinary houses were covered with flat roofs on which it was possible to walk and exchange news with the neighbors: Jesus enjoined upon his disciples the duty of proclaiming his gospel from the rooftops.[6] The word *tektōn* could also be applied to an artisan who worked in iron or stone. In brief, we may suppose that Joseph and later Jesus were good craftsmen in the village, well skilled in everything that concerned their trade.

1. Matt 13:55; Mark 6:3.
2. S. Safrai, "Education and the Study of the Torah," Safrai-Stern, 958.
3. Quoted in L. Deiss, *Printemps de la Liturgie* (Paris: Levain, 1979) 88. (*Springtime of the Liturgy*, trans. Matthew J. O'Connell [Collegeville, Minn.: The Liturgical Press, 1992].)
4. We must remember the manual trades were held in high esteem in Israel. Hillel the Elder (ca. 20 B.C.E.) was a journeyman. See Strack-Billerbeck, 2:745-746. Paul himself, with his friends Priscilla and her husband Aquila, made tents with material woven from goats' hair (See Acts 18:3).
5. G. Vermes, *Jésus le Juif*, Jésus et Jésus-Christ (Paris: Desclée de Brouwer, 1978) 26.
6. Matt 10:27; see Luke 12:3.

Joseph taught the child to recognize the various woods the Bible mentions and which he was to work with: oak, terebinth, plane, fir, cypress, poplar, sycamore, acacia, olive, mulberry, juniper. Oaks and terebinths, well known in sacred history, were often venerated as sacred trees. People remembered the oak of Moreh near Shechem where Abraham had stopped and the oak of Mamre at Hebron where he had erected an altar to Yahweh.[7] The terebinth at Ophrah, under which the angel of the Lord was unpretentiously sitting when he called Gideon to save his people, was famous.[8] Cedar and cypress had been used in the first Temple for the roof, the ceilings, the floors, the columns, and as a covering for the walls.[9] Olive wood was much valued—and still is today in Palestine—for sculptures. As for the sycamore, it was supposed to have extremely vigorous roots which penetrated even the rocks: when Jesus spoke of a faith capable of uprooting a sycamore and planting it in the sea,[10] he was speaking of a particularly strong faith.

Besides plows and yokes, Joseph and Jesus also made chests where winter cloaks, festive garments, and wedding robes were stored. These chests could also become hiding places for moths. Jesus spoke of certain treasured possessions which moths can destroy, whereas real treasures, those found in heaven, are imperishable.[11] We also think of woodwork like doors with their wooden latches and keys, the like of which are still found today in some Syrian villages. One could also bar the door with a piece of wood whose two ends could be inserted into the masonry either side of the door. In the parable of the ten bridesmaids, when the five foolish ones arrive late and want to enter the wedding hall, they find the door shut probably in this way.[12] Besides all these things, Joseph and Jesus probably made window shutters, tables, stools, lamp stands on which oil lamps were set—and all those who entered, Jesus said, saw the light.[13]

Joseph taught Jesus to safely handle the most commonly used tools: ax, saw, hammer, plane, various chisels. The ax was widely

7. Gen 12:6; 13:18.
8. Judg 6:11 (NRSV, "oak").
9. See 1 Kgs 6.
10. Luke 17:6 (NRSV, "mulberry"). See Strack-Billerbeck, 2:234-35.
11. Matt 6:20; Luke 12:33.
12. Matt 25:10.
13. Luke 8:16; Mark 4:21.

used, and Hebrew has several different words to designate ax and maul. We remember that John the Baptist, in his penitential preaching, declared that the ax was already lying at the root of every tree which would not produce "worthy fruit."[14] Indispensable for sculpture, the chisel was however regarded with suspicion because pious Jews feared it could be used to fashion idols.[15] Its use had been prohibited in the construction of the altar of Solomon's Temple.[16]

From Joseph, the child learned the value of work well done. For when one uses a T square or a ruler, no cheating is possible, no approximation allowed. Those who work with their hands "maintain the fabric of the world"[17] even though they are not cultivated. Joseph's work for daily bread taught the child the value of the effort to gain eternal life. Later on, Jesus remembered his work as a carpenter when he said in the synagogue at Capernaum, "Do not work for the food that perishes, but for the food that endures for eternal life."[18] His work as a carpenter and as the Messiah has really maintained the fabric of the world.

14. Matt 3:8; Luke 3:9.
15. Isa 44:9-20; Jer 10:3 ("chisel," according to the BJ); Bar 6:45; Wis 13:11-19.
16. Exod 20:15.
17. Sir 38:34.
18. John 6:27.

## JOSEPH THE RIGHTEOUS

In Matthew 1:19-20, where the angel tells Joseph to take Mary as his wife, Joseph is presented as a "righteous" man. It is important to understand this righteousness according to the meaning given it in the vocabulary of Matthew's Gospel. According to Matthew, Jesus had a piety built on a perfect observance of the Law, a righteousness which is allied with mercy and faithfulness and opens the doors of the reign.[1]

Joseph was righteous in his attitude toward Mary by respecting her mysterious motherhood whose origin he did not know.[2]

He was righteous in his attitude toward Jesus by wholeheartedly welcoming and raising the child whom heaven entrusted to him.

Now, at the heart of this education, there was what we call religious formation. Joseph's and Mary's familial intimacy was the environment where Jesus learned that there is a God of love who watches over the world, that this God is the father of tenderness and pity, that the first duty of all children of the Covenant is to love God with all one's heart and with all one's soul and with all one's mind and with all one's strength. Such is the paradoxical law of the incarnation: Joseph and Mary taught the love of God to the One who was the face of God's love on earth.

When a wise scribe—the very one who was not far from the reign of God[3]—asked Jesus, "Which commandment is the first of all?" Jesus answered by simply quoting the traditional text of Deuteronomy 6:4-5:

> Hear, O Israel: the Lord our God, the Lord is one; you shall love the Lord your God with all your heart, and with all your soul, and with all your mind, and with all your strength.[4]

1. Matt 5:6-7.
2. X. Léon-Dufour, *Etudes d'Evangile* (Paris: Seuil, 1965) 80–81, writes, "[Joseph] shows himself to be a righteous man . . . in that he does not want to pretend to be the father of the divine child."
3. Mark 12:34.
4. Mark 12:29-30, quoting Deut 6:4-5.
5. The French translation of the first blessing can be found in Deiss, *Printemps* 24–26, and the Latin translation of the three blessings in A. Hänggi and I. Pahl, *Prex Eucharistica* (Fribourg: Ed. Universitaires, 1968) 35–49.

This text is part of what is called the Shema Israel ("Hear, O Israel"). The Shema begins with two blessings,[5] continues with two texts from Deuteronomy (6:4-9, the beginning of which we just quoted, and 11:13-21) and a text from Numbers (15:37-41), and ends with a rather lengthy blessing. In fact, the whole Shema is considered a prayer, and this prayer is at the heart of Jewish piety. On the one hand, it proclaims the absolute oneness of God and, on the other, commands total faithfulness to the Covenant of love. Tradition explains with tenderness, "One first takes upon oneself the yoke of God's kinship, that is, one professes monotheism; then one takes on the yoke of the Law."[6]

People were (and still are) fond of stating that the practice of praying the Shema went back to an immemorial tradition: it is said the patriarch Jacob inaugurated it and Moses confirmed it later on.[7] In fact, the text of Deuteronomy is much more recent, although difficult to date. All we know is that the main documents constituting Deuteronomy were assembled before 622 B.C.E., the date of their discovery in the Temple at the time of Josiah's reform.[8] But this does not tell us at what date they were written. What is certain is that the recitation of the Shema had become traditional by the time of Jesus. It was (and still is) said morning and evening.[9] Its recitation was believed to be equivalent in God's eyes to the study of the Law day and night or to the offering of sacrifices in the Temple.[10]

The recitation of the Shema was obligatory for free men, but not for slaves, women, or children.[11] Its transmission to boys was the father's duty and therefore was incumbent on Joseph. Deuteronomy insists on this duty:

> Keep these words that I am commanding you today in your heart. Recite them to your children and talk about them when you are at home and when you are away, when you lie down and when you rise.[12]

---

6. Strack-Billerbeck, 4:189; H. Danby, *The Mishnah* (London: Oxford University Press, 1967) Berakoth 2:2, p. 3.

7. Strack-Billerbeck, 4:191-92.

8. L. Deiss, *Vivre la Parole en communauté* (Paris: Desclée de Brouwer, 1974) 83–95.

9. Strack-Billerbeck, 4:192.

10. Strack-Billerbeck, 4:190.

11. Ibid., 196–197.

12. Deut 6:6-7.

In fact, the Shema was the very first prayer Joseph taught the child. Tradition states, "As soon as a [male] child can speak, his father will teach him the Shema."[13] We can picture Joseph holding the little Jesus in his arms, or else placing him standing in front of him—people prayed standing[14]—turned toward Jerusalem,[15] slowly reciting the Shema with Mary. He would have accentuated the word *one* by prolonging it in order to emphasize it ("Hear, O Israel, Adonai our God, Adonai *one*") as custom demanded[16], and the little child would have stammered, as all young children do, the holy words, learning them by heart day after day. It was a unique family where the child from heaven received from his earthly father the Law come down from heaven.

Throughout his childhood, his adolescence, and his adulthood, Jesus progressed in the knowledge of what the Law of love required of him, and he marvelled at the ever new demands of the Shema. Like the Servant of Yahweh described in Isaiah, who declared, "Morning by morning he wakens / wakens my ear,"[17] Jesus discovered with each new dawn the way of love which the Father traced before him.

Jesus remained extremely discreet concerning this relationship of love with the Father, a relationship which formed the essence of his existence and which was at the heart of his peace and joy. In the Gospels he says only once that he loves the Father. This is just before the passion, during the discourse at the Last Supper, before he entered the way of suffering unto death, the way of no return:

> I do as the Father has commanded me, so that the world may know that I love the Father.[18]

In Psalm 63:4, the faithful one utters this cry of tenderness, "Your steadfast love is better than life." Or put another way, "For me, to love you, my God, is better than to live." This is exactly the mystery of Jesus' life. This "I love the Father," said before his death as a proof of his love, rejoins the "You will love the Lord your God" learned in Joseph's arms when Jesus was a little child.

13. Strack-Billerbeck, 4:196; Danby, *Mishnah*, Berakoth 4:5-6, p. 5.
14. Mark 11:25, "Whenever you stand praying. . . ." See R. de Vaux, *Les Institutions de l'Ancien Testament* (Paris: Cerf, 1958-60) 2:351-53.
15. See 1 Kgs 8:38; 2 Chr 6:34; Dan 6:10.
16. Strack-Billerbeck, 4:200.
17. Isa 50:4.
18. John 14:31.

## JOSEPH THE ICON OF THE HEAVENLY FATHER

Was Joseph a good father to Jesus? Let us say the word: Was he a good "daddy"?

The most beautiful and the truest thing we can say on this topic is that Joseph was so good, so tenderly lovable that as a child Jesus learned to discover in him the heavenly Father's image.

Indeed, Jesus dared to call God *Abba*. This Aramaic word, familiar and affectionate, is a child's expression whose equivalent would be our "daddy." As a child, Jesus gave this name to Joseph; later on, as an adult in possession of all his intellectual powers, he gave it to the Father in heaven in his most intimate prayers. It is as if this title, which expressed the fullness of the affection uniting him to his father on earth, now united him to his Father in heaven.

The title *Abba* given to God was new in the tradition of Israel. It is not found anywhere in the Old Testament and it is never a form of address to God in the Jewish literature of Jesus' time. "The sensibility of Jesus' contemporaries would have judged it disrespectful and even inconceivable to address God with this familiar word."[1] Jesus was the first to dare invoke God as the Abba in heaven. This term is part of the group of words called the *ipsissima vox* of Jesus, that is, his very word, his most authentic word, which tradition has preserved for us. It is found in the desolate prayer at Gethsemane as Mark's tradition records it:

> Abba, Father, for you all things are possible; remove this cup from me; yet, not what I want, but what you want.[2]

Some people think that this way of addressing God was in other prayers of Jesus[3] but that it disappeared when the Aramaic text was translated into Greek. "The study of the other formulas of Jesus' prayers to his Father, a study confirmed by the witness of the Aramaic versions, seems to clearly show that our Lord always invoked God with this Aramaic word *Abba*."[4] In particular, this is

---

1. J. Jeremias, *Théologie du Nouveau Testament*, Lectio Divina 76 (Paris: Cerf, 1973) 87. For a study of the word *abba*, see J. A. Fitzmeyer, "*Abba* and Jesus' Relation to God," *A cause de l'Evangile*, Lectio Divina 123 (Paris: Cerf, 1985) 15–38.

2. Mark 14:36.

3. For instance, in John 17:5, 21.

4. W. Narchel, *Abba, Père*, Analecta Biblica 19 (Rome: Biblical Institute Press, 1963) 145.

the case for the hymn of jubilation, "I thank you, Father, Lord of heaven and earth,"[5] and the Our Father according to Luke's tradition, "When you pray, say: Father."[6]

We recall that Luke's text of the Our Father is not identical with Matthew's which is longer.[7] Therefore, there existed different versions of the Lord's Prayer in the Greek-speaking communities of Antioch and the Aramaic-speaking communities of Jerusalem. This means that in the opinion of the Christian community, the exact wording of the Lord's Prayer was less important than its spirit. For according to the gospel, every Christian prayer must be, as it were, transfigured by this initial invocation, "Abba! Father!"

However, this invocation of familiar tenderness fully venerates God's transcendence and adores God's holy will. This is precisely why the fervent supplication of Jesus in Gethsemane, "Abba, Father," continues in a vein of adoration and humility, "yet, not what I want, but what you want."[8] Following Jesus' example, the Christian community learns that God's transcendence is the transcendence of God's fatherly love.

When families are not united, one does not dare speak of God as Father except with caution. Certain children may have negative images of their fathers: fathers who are alcoholic, given to anger, selfish. . . . In the Holy Family, the image of the father was nothing but one of kindness. Jesus remembered Joseph when he said:

> Is there anyone among you who, if your child asks for a fish, will give a snake instead of a fish? . . . If you then, who are evil, know how to give good gifts to your children, how much more will the heavenly Father give the Holy Spirit to those who ask him?[9]

Joseph's goodness must have shone radiantly for the child Jesus to have seen in it the heavenly Father's tenderness. Abba Joseph was for him the icon of the Abba in heaven. The discovery of the

5. Luke 10:21.

6. Luke 11:2.

7. In Matthew's tradition, 6:9-13, the Our Father contains seven petitions (three "heavenly" petitions and four "earthly" petitions). In Luke's tradition, 11:2-4, there are only five petitions (two "heavenly" and three "earthly"). The *Didache*, 8:2-3, whose earliest part was written at a time close to that of the redaction of the Gospels, quotes still another tradition of the Our Father.

8. Mark 14:36.

9. Luke 11:11, 13.

human tenderness Joseph lavished on him was the way to his discovery of the infinite tenderness the heavenly Father lavished on him.

The Gospels are extremely guarded on the topic of Jesus' psychological and spiritual development. We ourselves can approach only with respect this most secret sanctuary of his personality, where his affections, his desires, his loves resided; where his whole being was submissive to the heavenly Father. Now, the Gospels show us that Jesus loved children. Luke relates that even nurslings *(brephē)* were presented to him so he might touch them, "might lay his hands on them," as Matthew puts it.[10] He embraced children. He even embraced them too much in Matthew's and Luke's opinion: they omit this gesture of affectionate familiarity which might have tarnished, they feared, their Master's reputation. Only Mark dares to record this and he does it with insistence, twice.[11] Cannot we see in Jesus' gestures of tenderness for the little children the reflection of Joseph's tenderness for the child Jesus?

Only Jesus could give the name abba to his father Joseph. Jesus alone was the first to give his name Abba to his heavenly Father. After Jesus, through the Spirit that dwells in our hearts, we repeat with the first Christian generation the prayer "Abba! Father!"[12]

And we bless Joseph who, because of the tenderness God had placed in his heart for the child, was the initiator of Christian prayer.

10. Luke 18:15; Matt 19:13.
11. Compare Mark 9:36 with Matt 18:2 and Luke 9:47, and Mark 10:16 with Matt 19:15.
12. Rom 8:15; Gal 4:6.

## JOSEPH THE OBEDIENT

The Gospels do not relate any word of Joseph. In Mary's presence, as well as in Jesus', Joseph remained silent love. Even at the finding in the Temple he said nothing. And in God's presence this silent love became obedient love.

As the head of the family, Joseph was responsible for what we can call the family's "religious practice." Simple and joyous obedience was the rule.

Eight days after his birth, the child was circumcised according to the Law.[1]

Forty days after his birth, the child was presented in the Temple, "according to the law of Moses" or "as it is written in the law of the Lord."[2] And his parents, it is noted, accomplished "everything required by the law of the Lord."[3] It would be difficult to show more clearly faithfulness to the Law.

In order to keep the Holy Family away from Herod's persecution after the visit of the wise men from the East, "the angel of the Lord"[4] told Joseph to take his family and flee to Egypt. The angel also ordered the return to the "land of Israel" (Matt 2:13-23). We do not know what sources concerning these events were at Matthew's disposal. However, the narrative centers less on the historicity of the facts than on the fulfillment of the Scriptures. Three prophecies are quoted: that of Hosea (11:1), "Out of Egypt I have called my son" (Matt 2:15); that of Jeremiah (31:15) on Rachel weeping for her children (Matt 2:18); and last, "He will be called a Nazorean" (Matt 2:23), which was fulfilled by Joseph's settling in Nazareth. This third quotation, impervious to any philological, exegetical, or historical analysis,[5] probably comes from a source different from the one mentioning the angel of the Lord and the revelations in dreams.[6]

1. Luke 2:21.
2. Luke 2:22-23.
3. Luke 2:39.
4. The Old Testament expression "the angel of the Lord" can designate either a celestial messenger sent by God or God in person. For example, see Gen 16:10-13; 22:11-15.
5. According to E. Lohmeyer, *Das Evangelium des Matthäus* (Göttingen: Vandenhoeck and Ruprecht, 1958) 32.
6. G. M. Soares Prabhu, *The Formula Quotations in the Infancy Narrative of Matthew*, Analecta Biblica 63 (Rome: Biblical Institute Press, 1986) 215.

Joseph does not appear at the center of these stories. He is simply at the service of the child and his mother so that the Scriptures may be fulfilled. But Matthew—or his source—arranges the text according to a strict parallelism as if to highlight the perfection of Joseph's obedience:

> Get up, take the child and his mother, and flee to Egypt. . . . Then Joseph got up, took the child and his mother by night, and went to Egypt.[7]

The angel of the Lord appears to Joseph a second time and tells him to return to the land of Israel. We see here the same parallelism between the angel's order and Joseph's compliance:

> Get up, take the child and his mother and go to the land of Israel. . . . Then Joseph got up, took the child and his mother, and went to the land of Israel.[8]

Finally, "every year . . . for the festival of the Passover,"[9] that is, with a devout regularity, the Holy Family made the pilgrimage to Jerusalem. Furthermore, it was recommended that fathers accustom their children very early and gradually to the practice of the Law. The boys residing in Jerusalem were invited to go up in pilgrimage to the Temple as soon as they were able to hold their fathers' hands.[10] Jesus' pilgrimage to Jerusalem at the age of twelve is well in accordance with traditional piety.

What was the influence of Joseph's—and Mary's—obedience on the formation of the child Jesus? Did they, in the child's presence, speak about the "angel of the Lord" who visited Joseph three times?[11] Joseph is called "righteous."[12] As for Jesus, he is called "the Just One." The obedience of Jesus perfectly reflected the religious atmosphere of the family whose head was Joseph. Concerning his obedience to the heavenly Father, Jesus would declare later on, "I always do what is pleasing to him."[13]

7. Matt 2:13, 16.
8. Matt 2:20-21.
9. Luke 2:41-42.
10. Strack-Billerbeck, 2:144-46.
11. Matt 1:20; 2:13, 19.
12. Matt 1:19; Acts 7:52.
13. John 8:29.

## JOSEPH THE HUSBAND OF MARY

The love between a man and a woman, in its most intimate and profound aspect, always retains a certain mystery, as if it were at ease only in its most secret garden. Joseph's and Mary's love retains the most total mystery because it was lived in the most inviolable garden of their mutual tenderness. Only God, who was its author, knew this love. The Gospels speak to us of salvation history but reveal nothing of the intimate history of these two lovers who were unique in the whole world.

### Betrothal and Marriage

Mary is said to have been engaged *(emnēsteumenē)* to Joseph at the time of the annunciation according to Luke 1:27 and at the time of the announcement to Joseph *(mnēsteutheisē)* according to Matthew 1:18.[1]

In the Jewish cultural milieu of the time, betrothal had juridical force: it was considered a marriage before the spouses' cohabitation. If in the meantime the man died, the woman was regarded as a widow. If the betrothal was broken, the woman was sent away with a bill of divorce.[2]

For what reasons did Joseph choose young Miryam from among the girls of Nazareth to make her his bride? How did he begin to love her? Did he see in the eyes of this adolescent girl that part of heaven which dwelt in her immaculate heart? And how did Mary's father—Joachim according to tradition[3]—choose Joseph the righteous and entrust his daughter to him?

How old could Mary have been? Young girls were usually betrothed as soon as they became women. It was believed they reached puberty at about twelve or twelve and a half. Boys, it was believed, reached the age of puberty a year later. Marriage could take place one year after the betrothal.[4] In general, it was held that men could wait until the age of eighteen or twenty before marrying so that

1. Luke speaks of Mary as still being engaged to Joseph at the time of Jesus' birth in Bethlehem (2:5), in spite of the difficulty of interpretation that he thus creates.

2. Strack-Billerbeck, 1:51-53.

3. According to the Protoevangelium or Book of James, an apocryphal work of the second century, Mary's parents were named Anna and Joachim.

4. Strack-Billerbeck, 2:146, 374.

they would have time to build a house and plant a vineyard. People asserted that from God's heavenly throne, God observed men until their twentieth year to see whether they were taking a wife. But when the twenty years had elapsed and a man was not yet married, God was supposed to proclaim, "May his bones be scattered!"[5]

We remember how Matthew 1:18-19 narrates the conception of Jesus:

> Now the birth of Jesus the Messiah took place in this way. When his mother Mary had been engaged to Joseph, but before they lived together, she was found to be with child from the Holy Spirit. Her husband Joseph, being a righteous man and unwilling to expose her to public disgrace, planned to dismiss her quietly.

Here was the family established by God to welcome Salvation and bring it to the world: a young Galilean woman about fourteen, pregnant without her fiancé's knowing anything about it, and a young carpenter barely older than she. And when he noticed Mary's pregnancy, and was heavy-hearted about it, he resolved to dismiss her secretly in order not to harm her reputation since he continued to love her.

We know how the angel of Yahweh reassured him, "Joseph, son of David, do not be afraid to take Mary as your wife."[6] When Joseph woke up, did he go to see Mary? Did he take her two hands into his strong carpenter's hands? Did he look into her eyes full of virginal splendor in order to show her that he had understood everything—for in one way or another they had to speak about it together? And did he gently tell her, "Miryam, come to my home; we are getting married and my house is now yours"?

Matthew summarizes all of this love story with a solemn objectivity, "When Joseph awoke from sleep, he did as the angel of the Lord commanded him; he took her as his wife."[7] All is as crystal-clear as spring water, as objective and cold as a marriage contract. We shall learn nothing more.

Neither shall we learn anything concerning the wedding ceremony. In Jesus' time it lasted seven days. The principal rite was

5. This sentence goes back to Rabbi Jischmael (d. ca. 135), quoted in Strack-Billerbeck, 2:374. Certain similar sentences go back to the first century, according to S. Safrai, "Home and Family," Safrai-Stern, 755, n. 1.

6. Matt 1:20.

7. Matt 1:24.

the leading of the bride into her husband's house. The cortege formed in the evening and proceeded among songs, dances, blessings, and congratulations. When the bride was delayed, people liked to imagine that she found it hard to leave her parents because she loved them so much. . . . On this subject, Jesus told the parable of the nuptial procession arriving at midnight.[8]

The schools of Hillel and Shammai debated whether it was permitted to exaggerate in praise of the bride's beauty.[9] We may easily think that in practice it was permitted. Joseph must have thought that for once praise of the bride's beauty was not exaggerated.

One of the most significant rites was for the newlyweds to drink from the same cup.[10] When Joseph and Mary, in the midst of the customary cheering, shared the same cup, no one could have had any idea of how intimately their destinies were blended—more than the wine in the nuptial cup—or that a child, already present in the bride's womb, was the foundation of their love.

We may surmise that Joseph surrounded Mary with faithful attentiveness throughout the course of her pregnancy. Mary experienced the hidden beginning of an unborn human being in its mother's womb. She felt the first signs of her child's presence, his first movements. And Jesus, like all babies, very early recognized the sound of Mary's voice. One morning, smiling, she may have said to Joseph, "I felt the baby move inside me." Is it not a joy which all wives share with their husbands? And Joseph may have given one of those banal answers to which warm-hearted men have recourse to hide their tenderness, "Miryam, you are marvelous." But nothing of the kind is to be found in the Gospels. Luke prefers to mention John the Baptist's leap of joy in the womb of his mother Elizabeth and the praise which Elizabeth then addressed to Mary, "Blessed are you among women, and blessed is the fruit of your womb."[11] This is the only word the Gospels have about Jesus in Mary's womb.

8. Matt 25:6. In Matthew's parable, it is not the woman who comes into her betrothed's house, but the man who arrives in the middle of the night. This arrival at midnight reflects the tradition of Jewish messianic hope, according to which the Messiah was to come, it was believed, in the middle of Passover night. See R. Le Déaut, *La nuit pascale*, Analecta Biblica 22 (Rome: Biblical Institute Press, 1963) 279-98.

9. Safrai, "Home and Family," 758.

10. S. Hanson, "Hochzeit," *Biblisch-historisches Wörterbuch*, ed. B. Reicke and L. Rost (Göttingen: Vandenhoeck and Ruprecht, 1962-) 22:731.

11. Luke 1:42.

## Joseph in Bethlehem

Joseph's presence at Jesus' birth is mentioned with extreme discretion. However, Joseph was the witness of this birth which is at the center of the history of the world. At the beginning of the story, we learn that Joseph "went from the town of Nazareth in Galilee to Judea, to *the city of David* called Bethlehem, because he was descended from the house and *family of David.* He went to be registered with Mary to whom he was engaged and who was expecting a child."[12] Jesus, who is invoked later on in the Gospels as "son of David," was born in Bethlehem, *the city of David,* thanks to Joseph who was descended from *the house of David.*

Joseph is not named within the narrative of Jesus' birth. Once again, we feel the need to celebrate the marvelous humility of Joseph. We may surmise that his distress at not finding room for his wife in the village of his kinsfolk was extreme. Luke writes, "There was no place for them in the inn."[13] This sentence can also be understood as meaning, "The inn was not the place for them"[14] because an inn is not an appropriate place to give birth. Jesus was born somewhere, on the way, in the wind, under the stars, in a cave used as a stable (the word *phatnē* is used three times).[15] The destitution in which Jesus was born foretold the poverty of him who later on would not have even a stone on which to lay his head.[16]

What can a carpenter do for his wife in labor? We may suppose that Joseph cleaned the stable as best he could, arranged the manger in which Mary would place the newborn. Luke relates:

> While they were there, the time came for her to deliver her child. And she gave birth to her firstborn son and wrapped him in bands of cloth, and laid him in a manger.[17]

Before laying the child in the manger, Mary probably placed him tenderly in Joseph's arms while whispering, "He is your child." Is this not what all mothers do?

12. Luke 2:4-5.
13. Luke 2:7.
14. E. Delebecque, trans., *Evangile de Luc* (Klincksieck, 1992) 13. See also the note on Luke 2:7, p. 12.
15. Luke 2:7, 12, 16.
16. Luke 9:58.
17. Luke 2:7-8.

Every birth is a woman's triumphant fruit-bearing, the victory of human love over death. Moreover, this birth was God's unheard-of fruit-bearing in the world. But not one word of emotion, still less of exaltation, is in the text. The coming of the King of Glory among human beings is told with simple words speaking of swaddling clothes and a manger. And the epiphany of the One whom angels acclaimed as "Savior . . . Messiah, the Lord,"[18] who is the center of world history, had for witnesses only a young Galilean woman and a poor carpenter. To whom we must add the donkey which in Palestine was part of all journeys and which kept looking at its manger where the little Jesus was resting.

We find Joseph mentioned at the end of the story of the birth. Angels, "a multitude of the heavenly host,"[19] celebrated the newborn king, announced peace to those whom God loves, aroused the shepherds who came running to marvel at the infant: "So they went with haste and found Mary and Joseph, and the child lying in the manger."[20] Joseph played his role of husband and father toward Mary and the child. But the world cannot guess anything of the mystery they lived together.

18. Luke 2:11.
19. Luke 2:13.
20. Luke 2:16.

## JOSEPH AND THE EVER-VIRGIN

Ignatius of Antioch (d. ca. 110) states that "the prince of this world was ignorant of Mary's virginity and childbearing, as well as of the Lord's death, three mysteries accomplished in God's silence."[1] Today the world still cannot understand the mystery of the perpetual virginity of Mary. Christian faith venerates Mary as the *Aeiparthenos*, the "Ever-Virgin."[2]

Joseph and Mary were a real couple. Now, one does not get married with the intention of abstaining from sexual relations and thus not having children. Sexual relations are an integral part of the conjugal relation. Even the most sublime and spiritual love is rooted in the humility of the flesh. Children are the divine blessing founded on love.[3] Even in the New Testament, sterility is regarded as a humiliation: when Elizabeth became pregnant with John, she declared that the Lord had taken away the disgrace she endured among the people. Then at John's birth "her neighbors and relatives heard that the Lord had shown his great mercy to her."[4] Under these conditions, how can we understand Joseph's marriage with the Ever-Virgin? Did they even discuss the subject? Perhaps there was never any conversation on this point. Between people who love one another a simple look can be more eloquent than a long discourse. After the angel's visit, first to Mary, then to Joseph; after the birth of the child and the angels' songs in Bethlehem; after the marvelous events of the Magi's journey from the East and the presentation in the Temple, they may have understood that in Jesus the fecundity of their love was fulfilled beyond every human hope. No one heard their conversation. No one glimpsed the beloved's look at his beloved. No one can enter the mystery of their love or imagine their intimacy.

What name can be given to such a marriage? We did not find any suitable name for Joseph's fatherhood. Would there be any suit-

1. *Lettre aux Ephésiens* (19:1), Sources chrétiennes 10 (Paris: Cerf, 1958) 88.

2. The term *aei-parthenos* is attested at the beginning of the fourth century in Epiphanius of Salamis. See Denzinger-Schönmetzer, n. 44. On Jesus' brothers and sisters, see ch. 6, pp. 144–149.

3. Tradition required the man who after ten years of marriage did not yet have any children to divorce his wife and take another wife. See Safrai, "Home and Family," 750.

4. Luke 1:25, 58.

able name for his marriage? Indeed, sexual desire between spouses is a wholesome thing willed by God. How was it lived in this marriage? We know nothing at all about it. When evoking the nature of human love in heaven and the difficulty of imagining it, Jesus said to the Sadducees, "You [do not] know . . . the power of God."[5] How could we not respect this power of God which was at work in the love of Joseph and Mary?

Tradition likes to assert that Jesus' birth consecrated Mary's virginal body.[6] Now, Joseph's destiny was linked with Mary's. Joseph shared in the consecration of Mary's body. Willed by God, their marriage had united them in "one flesh";[7] it realized the perfection of "what God has joined together"[8] on earth. In a certain way their nuptial love became like that between Adam and Eve in paradise, that is, it reached the spiritual fullness to which God calls a man and woman when joining them together. It became also a prophecy of the eternal love that is the lifeblood of the reign of the resurrection. A love that never knew the wound of sin, but only the kiss of grace. A love that was never the selfish possession of the beloved, but only a pure self-oblation. A love that kept all the riches of the sexual difference, but transfigured them into gifts of grace. Finally, a love that realized the ideal of what God, in God's Word, proclaimed concerning marriage.

With what loving eyes Joseph looked on Mary when they read Proverbs together:

> He who finds a wife finds a good thing
> and obtains favor from the LORD.[9]

It is not just that Joseph had found Mary; God had given her to him for his wife. And this gift was not only the grace *(charis)* of a woman, but of the woman "full of grace" *(kecharitomenē)* according to the angel's salutation.

---

5. Mark 12:24. As a mere hypothesis, we may suppose in this marriage a grace similar to that of the charism of total fast, a charism found in our own time, for example in Anne Catherine Emmerich, Theresa Neumann, Marthe Robin, all of whom lived for several decades without taking any food.

6. Dogmatic Constitution on the Church *(Lumen Gentium)* no. 57: "Jesus has not diminished but consecrated her virginal integrity" ("virginalem ejus integritatem non minuit, sed sacravit").

7. Gen 2:24.

8. Matt 19:6.

9. Prov 18:22.

Had Joseph been told of Elizabeth's cry when she welcomed Mary, "Blessed are you among women"?[10] Did he understand that Mary was as blessed as Jael[11] had been, who had triumphed over Sisera the Canaanite at the time of the cruel battles of the Judges' era, or as Judith[12] had been, who had vanquished the impious Holofernes? Mary's motherhood continued the history of Israel's battles: it was the victory over the powers hostile to Yahweh. And he, Joseph, was the ally of the victorious woman. If Mary was the woman blessed among all women, was he not, he too, blessed among all husbands?

One day, in the synagogue of Nazareth, the passage assigned had been, in accordance with the calendar of the readings of the Law, this text from Deuteronomy:

> If you heed these ordinances, by diligently observing them, the LORD your God . . . will love you, bless you, and multiply you; he will bless the fruit of your womb.[13]

Joseph had obeyed. God had blessed his bride's virginal womb. Inspired by the Holy Spirit, Elizabeth had attested that the prophecy from Deuteronomy was accomplished in Mary to whom she had said, "Blessed is the fruit of your womb."[14]

How could Joseph's heart not melt with tenderness when he remembered, all the while planing away at his wood, this biblical love song:

> Let your fountain be blessed,
>> and rejoice in the wife of your youth.
>> a lovely deer, a graceful doe. . . .
>> may you be intoxicated always by her love.[15]

Had he not found in Mary, together with the joy of his life, the presence of Emmanuel, God with him?

What did he think when he read this other maxim of wisdom inspired by the Holy Spirit:

10. Luke 1:42.
11. Judg 5:24.
12. Jdt 13:18.
13. Deut 7:12-13.
14. Luke 1:42.
15. Prov 5:18-19.

> A woman's beauty lights up a man's face,
>> and there is nothing he desires more.
> If kindness and humility mark her speech,
>> her husband is more fortunate than other
>>> men.[16]

Mary had been the strongest of his desires as a man. And she, who was all gentleness and kindness, had made him "more fortunate than other men."

In the couple Joseph and Mary God realized God's dream of love between a man and a woman. In order to create Eve, God took a rib—a part of his heart, as we would say today—from Adam and out of it made the first woman. In order to create Mary, God made Joseph's heart and joined it to that of Jesus' mother. Joseph's heart must have been very beautiful to give birth to so many wonders in Mary's heart. People often say of two persons in love that they have received their hearts from one another. Mary received her heart from Joseph. Joseph received his from Mary. They built their home by placing their two hearts in God's hand.

Scripture also says:

> A loyal wife brings joy to her husband,
>> and he will complete his years in peace.
> A good wife is a great blessing;
>> she will be granted among the blessings
>>> of the man who fears the LORD.
> Whether rich or poor, his heart is content,
>> and at all times his face is cheerful.[17]

Joseph lived in material poverty and even in want during the exile in Egypt. But he was rich with this joy that nourishes the heart and that only a cherished spouse can give to his or her companion, rich with this peace only God could give him by joining him with Mary.

"It is not good that the man should be alone."[18] It was not good that Mary should be alone for Jesus' birth in Bethlehem. It was not good that she should be alone when both father and mother were

16. Sir 36:27-28.
17. Sir 26:2-4.
18. Gen 2:18.

needed for the awakening of his intelligence and the formation of his affective equilibrium. It was not good that she should be alone at the time of her son's crisis of adolescence. It was good that Joseph should share her devotion to Jesus. It was good also that Mary should embrace Joseph in the arms of her tenderness and should make him fully happy to be the head of the Holy Family.

# Chapter 2
# Mary and Jesus

## SOURCES

### The Gospel Data

**W**hat are the biblical sources which allow us to probe the relationship of Mary with her child Jesus?

*Mark* represents the oldest tradition. This tradition does not say anything at all about the childhood years. Jesus appears all of a sudden, fully mature, to receive John's baptism.[1] Therefore, from the time of the resurrection to that of the destruction of Jerusalem[2]—that is, some forty years—it was possible to proclaim Jesus' universal lordship without saying one word about his birth and childhood. However, Mark knows well the earthly kinship of Jesus, "the carpenter, the son of Mary."[3] But he seems still more concerned about stressing that Jesus' kinship, according to God, is made up of all those who accomplish the will of the Father.[4]

*John* begins his Gospel with the hymn to the eternal Word who "was with God" "in the beginning."[5] This allows him to declare later

---

1. Mark 1:9.
2. Mark does not allude at all to this event. Therefore, some authors assume that the redaction of his Gospel is before this date.
3. Mark 6:3. Mark never mentions the name of Joseph, "father" of Jesus. It is supposed that Joseph had died by the time Jesus began his ministry.
4. Mark 3:31-35.
5. John 1:1.

on that Jesus "came down from heaven."[6] Nevertheless, he strongly maintains the realism of the incarnation: "And the Word became flesh."[7] Such a theology in which Jesus "comes down" from heaven obviously imparts no information on his childhood.

Only Matthew and Luke present stories about Jesus' childhood,[8] each one according to the sources at his disposal and his charism as evangelist.

*Matthew* writes narratives that remain guarded on the historical plane, but are very rich on the theological plane. They have as their background prophecies and remembrances of the Exodus. Mary is shown as the virgin who gave birth to Emmanuel according to Isaiah 7:14, quoted in the Greek of the Septuagint. Matthew likes to emphasize Joseph's vocation. He is the one who receives communications from heaven, presented in three "dreams," by the "angel of the Lord." Throughout the story, there is no dialogue, not even a word said by either Joseph or Mary. Their only response is obedience to God, the master of history. In this theological garden, it is difficult to picture Mary's relationship with her child, Emmanuel.

Luke is the only one who supplies us with basic texts, that is,
—the annunciation (1:26-38),
—the visitation to Elizabeth (1:39-56),
—the birth in Bethlehem and the circumcision (2:1-21),
—the presentation of Jesus in the Temple (2:22-38),
—the childhood in Nazareth (2:39-40),
—Jesus in the Temple among the teachers (2:41-50),
—the hidden life in Nazareth (2:51-52).

Luke wrote these texts with a historian's honesty. He conducted his research on the events "carefully"[9] as he tells us in the prologue

6. John 3:13; 6:33, 38, 41, 42, 50, 58. John preserves only two words said by Mary during Jesus' public life: "They have no wine" (2:3) and "Do whatever he tells you" (2:5). The second is probably a citation of the word of Pharaoh ordering the Egyptians to do whatever Joseph told them (Gen 41:55). In the Samaritan tradition, Joseph was venerated as a king (see P.-E. Boismard, *Moïse ou Jésus* [Leuven: University Press, 1988] 34–38). Consequently, Jesus appears as the new king who supplies the wine for the wedding feast as Joseph had supplied bread.

7. John 1:14.

8. On the relationship between the narratives of Matthew and Luke, see R. E. Brown, *The Birth of the Messiah* (New York: Doubleday, 1977), and R. Laurentin, *Les Evangiles de l'enfance du Christ* (Paris: Desclée et Desclée de Brouwer, 1982). On the quotations in Matthew 1-2, see Prabhu, *Formula Quotations*.

9. Luke 1:3, *akribōs*.

to his Gospel. He intended his stories to be received not as pious imaginings but as historical narratives. From what source did he draw them?

Especially when it is a question of events as intimate as the virginal conception, the source could have been only Mary herself. After the annunciation, Mary must have shared the weight of this mystery first of all with her mother. A young girl of thirteen or fourteen, she could undertake the journey to visit her relative Elizabeth only with her mother's consent. Elizabeth also must have been informed since she welcomed Mary by calling her "the mother of my Lord."[10] This mystery was kept secret, as a family treasure. Indeed, throughout his entire life Jesus seemed to be "Joseph's son," "the carpenter's son."[11] The revelation of a conception by the work of "the holy Spirit" and by "the power of the Most High" would have served to elicit nothing but derision from Jesus' enemies. It was probably only after the resurrection or even Mary's death that the mystery of Jesus' origins could be shared with the primitive community. It was there that Luke was able to obtain what has been called "Mary's memoirs." But we do not know how close the first Greek translation was to the Hebrew or Aramaic original, neither do we know how close the text Luke reproduces in his Gospel is to this pre-Lukan translation. Analysis can detect traces of the Aramaic, the Hebrew, the Septuagint, and Luke's literary mannerisms.[12] But it can neither retrace with complete surety the path from Luke back to Mary nor find again in all their freshness the words which Mary actually spoke.

## The Magnificat

Among all the texts Luke presents to us, the most important is the Magnificat: it allows us to tentatively enter into Mary's heart and get some idea of the influence of the mother on the child. Here is the literary outline of the Magnificat, with the Old Testament quotations written in italics.

---

10. Luke 1:43. We are adopting the hypothesis of P. Gaechter, *Maria im Erdenleben* (Innsbrück: Tyrolia, 1953) 62, 102.

11. Luke 4:22; Matt 13:55.

12. On the Hebraisms and Aramaisms in Luke's Greek text, see M.-J. Lagrange, *Evangile selon Saint Luc*, Etudes Bibliques (Paris: Gabalda, 1927) ciii–cx.

|  | Luke 1:46-55 | Sources |
|---|---|---|
| 46 | *My soul* magnifies *the Lord,* | Ps 35:9; Hab 3:18; |
| 47 | and my spirit *rejoices* <br> in *God my Savior,* | 1 Sam 2:1; Isa 61:10 |
| 48 | for *he has looked with favor* on <br> *the lowliness of his servant.* <br> Surely, from now on all generations <br> *will call me blessed;* | 1 Sam 1:11 <br><br><br> Gen 30:13; Mal 3:12 |
| 49 | for the Mighty One *has done great* <br> *things* for me, <br> and *holy is his name.* | Deut 10:21 <br><br> Ps 111:9; 1 Sam 2:2 |
| 50 | His *mercy* is for those <br> *who fear him* <br> *from generation to generation.* | Ps 103:17 <br> Ps 103:1 <br> Ps 103:17 |
| 51 | He has shown *strength with his arm;* <br> *he has scattered the proud* in the <br> thoughts of their hearts. | Ps 89:11 |
| 52 | *He has brought down* the powerful <br> from their *thrones,* <br> and lifted up *the lowly;* | Sir 10:14-15; <br> Job 12:19; <br> 1 Sam 2:6-8 |
| 53 | *He has filled* the hungry *with* <br> *good things,* <br> and sent *the rich* away empty. | Pss 107:9; 34:10;[13] <br> 1 Sam 2:5 |
| 54 | *He has helped* his *servant Israel,* <br> *in remembrance of his mercy,* | Isa 41:8, 10 |
| 55 | according to the promise he made <br> to *our ancestors,* <br> to *Abraham* and to *his* <br> *descendants forever.* | Mic 7:20; Isa 41:8; <br> 2 Sam 22:51 |

When we peruse this text with its light-filled archaisms, we cannot but see most clearly that Mary's canticle, which is the thanksgiving song par excellence in the New Testament, is made up of reminiscences from the Old Testament to such an extent that strictly speaking, it does not contain one single original sentence.[14] The origi-

13. Hebrew: "the young lions"; Greek: "the rich."

14. One finds a listing of quotations in R. Laurentin, *Court Traité sur la Vierge Marie,* 5th ed. (Paris: Lethielleux, 1967) 169, and in R. E. Brown, *Birth of the Messiah,* 358–59. This listing varies from author to author, depending on how one takes into account implicit quotations, especially numerous in Luke's infancy narratives (chs. 1–2).

nality of Mary's praise, its astounding newness, is this: in her, the Old Testament acclaims the Saving God of the New Testament.

Who composed this quilt of biblical texts? Some have thought it might have been an already-existing psalm originating either in the circles of "the poor of Yahweh" or else a victory song going back to Maccabean times.[15] According to these, Mary or the Greek translator or Luke himself would have developed or adapted it. Others have suggested a Johannine or Judeo-Christian origin. According to these, Luke would have put the words into Mary's mouth. Such redactional work was not beyond what an evangelist could accomplish under the Holy Spirit's inspiration.

It is also possible to suppose—and it is the simplest hypothesis, that of Luke—that the text was composed by Mary herself. Jesus' mother belonged to a people whose prayer book was, preeminently, memory. This stream of praise and thanksgiving sprang from the treasury of her memory nourished by the Word.

The Magnificat is so much of one piece with the stories of the annunciation and the visitation that one cannot extract it from them without dismembering the text. Indeed, when Mary declares that God has looked with favor on the lowliness of his *servant* (1:48), she herself makes the reference to the answer she had given to the angel at the annunciation, "Here am I, the *servant* of the Lord" (1:38).

When she sings that all generations will call her *blessed* (1:48), she echoes the joyful salutation which Elizabeth has just greeted her with, "And *blessed* is she who believed" (1:45).

When she proclaims that the Mighty One *(dunatos)* has done great things for her (1:49), she echoes Gabriel, who affirmed that nothing is impossible *(adunatēsei)* with God (1:37). At the same time, this word recalls that the God of Abraham, when promising the Covenant, revealed God to Sarah as the wonder-worker for whom nothing is impossible *(adunatei)* (Gen 18:14). Daughter of Sarah, heiress to the Covenant, Mary sings in her song of thanksgiving precisely the fulfillment of this Covenant "according to the promise he made . . . to Abraham and to his descendants forever."

Lastly, at the very beginning of the Magnificat, Mary indicates the meaning of the name of Jesus, which means Savior (Matt 1:21).

15. A. George, *Etudes l'Evangile de Luc*, Sources Bibliques (Paris: Gabalda, 1978) 442.

She declares that she rejoices in God, her *Savior,* that is, in this Jesus whom she is carrying.[16]

Therefore, the Magnificat fits perfectly in Luke's infancy narratives.[17] We are justified in thinking that it faithfully represents what Mary was like. Indeed, Jesus' mother was well known in the early community. Luke takes pleasure in explicitly mentioning her presence at the first Pentecost (ca. 30), as well as that of his "brothers," that is, a group of relatives.[18] Now, the final version of Luke's Gospel, with the infancy narratives, is certainly later than the fall of Jerusalem in 70 and probably earlier than the 90s; that is, it dates from forty to sixty years after the first Pentecost.[19] We can speculate that there were still eyewitnesses at that time—perhaps even some of the persons Luke calls Jesus' "brothers"—who had personally known his mother; besides, there would have been a fair number of people who had known these eyewitnesses well. The portrait Luke paints of Mary forty or sixty years after the first Pentecost—which corresponds to the stretch between two generations, or to the time which separates a grandchild from its grandparents—must have been substantially faithful to the image of Mary tradition had preserved. Otherwise, the Christian community would never have accepted Luke's text. In other words, the Magnificat is the genuine mirror of Mary's soul. It was only later, when all witnesses were dead, that the apocryphal writers would set to work and that, in the second century, the author of the Book of James or Protoevangelium would compose a slender book about Mary full of strange marvels. But this book would never be regarded as a Gospel.

16. See Laurentin, *Evangiles de l'Enfance,* 209–10 (etymological allusions to people's names in Luke 1–2).

17. H. Schürmann, *Das Lukasevangelium,* Herders Kommentar, Band 3, Teil 1 (1969) 141. Even if one attributes the Magnificat to Mary, one can accept that it was inserted later on into the original story of the visitation. The evidence for this is that whereas Elizabeth greets Mary and proclaims her "blessed," Mary does not respond at all to her cousin's greeting, which is "contrary to all good manners" (Gaetcher). And after the Magnificat, when it is said that she "remained with her," we must understand "with Elizabeth," who has not been named for 9 verses (see Gaechter, *Maria im Erdenleben,* 40–42).

18. Acts 1:14.

19. This final edition presents older pre-Synoptic material, especially in the section of the journey to Jerusalem (9:51–18:14). See L. Deiss, *Synopse des quatre Evangiles* (Paris: Desclée de Brouwer, 1991) 339.

Is it possible to detect, as if following a trail, the influence that Mary may have had on the child Jesus? This is what we propose to do and here is how we might proceed.

In the Magnificat, we discover a certain number of biblical themes. We also find these same themes in Jesus' life and preaching.

Of course, Mary and Jesus may have independently discovered these themes in Scripture and tradition. But is it not also possible to think that like all mothers, Mary naturally influenced her child and that his religious formation bears the imprint of her own piety?

The mystery remains untouched. We do not know to what depth familial influence marked Jesus' soul. Nor do we know how Jesus himself, as his personality developed, deepened his relationship with the heavenly Father or how the piety learned and practiced in Nazareth finally led him to the folly of the cross. This relationship remains Jesus' secret garden into which only the Father had access. For our part, to know that the tenderness of a man and woman, who lived in the simplicity of Nazareth, contributed to building up the personality of the One our faith acclaims as the Lord of eternal ages is enough to nurture our wonderment and praise.

## A SOUL FULL OF PRAISE

### Mary's Praise

> My soul magnifies the Lord,
> and my spirit rejoices
> in God my Savior. (Luke 1:46)

Mary was a soul full of praise. With the opening words of the Magnificat, the essential is said. No entreaty, no supplication. Nothing but exultation, jubilation, the celebration of God's salvation.

The first part of the Magnificat is circumscribed by a literary inclusion[1] based on the verb *megalunein* ("magnify," 1:46) and the adjective *megala* ("great things," 1:49). Translations labor to render the play on words which is so obvious in Greek. We could say that Mary *magnifies* the Lord because the Lord has done *magnificent things* for her. Or else, Mary *marvels* because her God has worked *marvels* for her.

In this first part, Mary commemorates (we could say "makes anamnesis of" as in a liturgical celebration) the marvelous gifts lavished on her by God. Now, all these marvels are, as it were, gathered into one, her motherhood, that is, this Jesus she is carrying in her womb. Mother of Jesus: is this not the whole of her very long story? The old Latin translation (the Vulgate) of the song of Habakkuk, a text akin to the Magnificat, felicitously renders the meaning of the original:

> I will rejoice in the Lord,
> I will exult in God, my Savior *[in Deo Jesu meo]*.[2]

Another cause of exultation for Mary is the loving look which God casts on the lowly. It was Hannah in the Old Testament, the barren woman, Elkanah's wife, who opened the way of praise for Mary. The episode took place during the bleak period of the Judges, around 1050. In the ancient sanctuary of Shiloh, Hannah was pouring out the bitterness of her soul and imploring, "O LORD of hosts, if only you will look on the *misery* [lowliness] of your servant, and *remember* me and not forget your servant, but will give your ser-

---

1. A literary device in which a word or phrase used at the beginning of a section is repeated at its end.
2. Hab 3:18.

vant a male child. . . ."[3] And God remembered Hannah. God looked with favor on the lowliness of God's servant. She became the mother of the little Samuel. She sang the very first Magnificat:

> My heart exults in the LORD. . . .
> I rejoice in my victory. . . .
> There is no holy One like the LORD.[4]

Mary knew and loved Hannah's prayer. She borrowed her words when she sang of the Lord who "has looked with favor on the *lowliness* of his servant" and who *remembered* "his mercy." With Mary, Hannah therefore leaves the ancient sanctuary of Shiloh, enters the Church of the New Testament, and acclaims Christ Jesus. In this song of praise addressed to the God of the lowly, Samuel's mother and Jesus' mother are the soloists who, in their immense song, lead the choir of all the lowly of the earth.

Of the little Samuel, it is said that he was growing "both in stature and in favor with the LORD.[5] Of the little Jesus, it is similarly said that he "increased in wisdom and in years, and in divine and human favor."[6] Samuel was *an* exceptional prophet among other prophets announcing the messianic times. Jesus was *the* prophet of the messianic times. Samuel's mother and Jesus' mother are sisters when they sing the God of the lowly.

The first part of the Magnificat (1:46-49 is an "I-section." Mary gives thanks for her personal history. The second part (1:50-54), like the first, is defined by an inclusion based on the word *eleos* ("mercy") which appears in verse 50: "His *mercy* is for those who fear him / from generation to generation." The same word occurs again in verse 54: "in remembrance of his *mercy*." In this second part, Mary celebrates the deeds which the Lord has accomplished in favor of Abraham and his descendants. In a litany of praise, the verbs cluster and chime as on Easter morning: God has scattered the proud, brought down the powerful, lifted up the lowly, fed the hungry, sent away the rich empty-handed, helped Israel. All these verbs are in the aorist tense, the tense without boundaries (*aoristos*, "without borders"), not simply to indicate that God accomplished

---

3. 1 Sam 1:11.
4. 1 Sam 2:1-2.
5. 1 Sam 2:26.
6. Luke 2:52.

these wonders in the past. For here this unbounded tense is a gnomic aorist—it designates "an action applicable to all times,"[7] as if one was affirming a question of principle: Here is what God's mercy has done in the past. Here is what it continues to accomplish in the present. And here is how it will continue to act in eternity. Therefore, Mary's praise encompasses the whole of sacred history. This history, from its origins until the dawn of the last morning, is entirely enclosed within God's mercy.

The text that most closely inspired Mary's praise is Psalm 103; it is probably the most admirable in the whole Book of Psalms. It celebrates the God of Sinai, "merciful and gracious, slow to anger and abounding in love."[8] The antiphon, "Bless the LORD, O my soul," is a prelude and conclusion to the psalm. It holds the celebration of the God of love as with both hands and surrounds it with praise. The points of contact between the psalm and the Magnificat are obvious:

| Psalm 103 | Luke 1 |
|---|---|
| Bless the LORD, O my soul,<br>    and all that is within me,<br>bless his holy name (v. 1). | My soul magnifies the LORD (v. 46)<br>and holy is his name (v. 49). |
| But the steadfast love of the<br>    LORD is from everlasting to<br>    everlasting<br>  on those who fear him (v. 17). | His mercy is for those who<br>    fear him<br>  from generation to<br>    generation (v. 50). |

In Mary's Magnificat, it is the theme of mercy which forms the inclusion (vv. 50 and 54). In Psalm 103, it is the theme of praise (vv. 1 and 22). Mary's praise, like that of the Psalm, is directed to God's merciful love which rests upon those who fear God.

Does this Magnificat reveal a momentary piety—at the visitation—or does it express an entire life of praise? Did it mark Jesus' piety? Was the child Jesus schooled by his mother's praise?

### Jesus' Praise

I thank you, Father,
Lord of heaven and earth (Luke 10:21).

7. F. Blass, *Grammatik des neutestamentlichen Griechisch*, 10th ed., ed. A. Debrunner (Göttingen: Vandenhoeck & Ruprecht, 1959) n. 333.
8. Ps 103:8; Exod 34:6-7.

Let us rephrase the question: What believers, having discovered God's mercy in their lives and celebrating it in their praise, would not wish to attract their brothers and sisters to share in this praise? What mother—especially if she is called Mary—would not wish to invite her child into it? The psalmist, singing "I will bless the LORD at all times," immediately adds "O magnify the LORD *with me,* / and let us exalt his name *together.*"[9]

Therefore, there is a solidarity in praise. The hymns of Qumran speak of "a community of jubilation."[10] We may suppose that the Holy Family formed such a community.

In order to say that Mary rejoiced, Luke uses the verb *agalliasthai* ("rejoice," "exalt," "thrill with joy"). Now, Luke knows well the nuances of words. He uses this verb no place else in his Gospel save once, precisely to characterize Jesus' exultation in what is called the hymn of jubilation (10:21-22).

The introduction to this hymn is remarkable. It is proper to Luke.[11] It says, "At that same hour Jesus *rejoiced* in the Holy Spirit."[12] In the same way Mary's spirit *rejoices* in God her Savior, Jesus *rejoices* in his spirit. And he blesses his Father:

> I thank you, Father, Lord of heaven and earth, because you have hidden these things from the wise and the intelligent and have revealed them to infants; yes, Father, for such was your gracious will.

We have here the highest and most significant prayer of what we could call Jesus' religion. It is praise and blessing of the Father, adoration of God's benevolence. The hymn of jubilation is for Jesus what the Magnificat is for Mary. As with Mary, the reason for this praise is the benevolence of the Father toward little ones,[13] those Mary calls the lowly. This "yes, Father," uttered in jubilation of heart, announces the humble entreaty at Gethsemane:

9. Ps 34:3.

10. Hymns III:23 and XI:14. See J. Carmignac and P. Guibert, *Les textes de Qumrân* (Paris: Letouzey et Ané, 1961) 1:200, 256.

11. The parallel text in Matthew 11:25 presents only a vague "at that time."

12. Most versions have "in the holy spirit" and the translations render "in the Holy Spirit," which was Luke's theology. But a very early papyrus, P 45, going back to the third century, simply says "in the spirit," which could be the most ancient text.

13. The "little ones" are those whom the Qumran community regarded as "the simple ones." Jesus blesses his Father because "the divine revelation is now granted, no longer to the wise and intelligent, but precisely to these *nēpioi* ("little ones," "infants"). J. Dupont, *Etudes sur les Evangiles synoptiques* (Leuven: University Press, 1985) 590.

> Abba, Father, for you all things are possible; remove this cup from
> me; yet not what I want, but what you want.[14]

The "for you all things are possible" of Gethsemane echoes the
"nothing will be impossible with God" of Nazareth. And the "not
what I want, but what you want" reminds us of Mary's answer,
"let it be with me according to your word."

Therefore, there is a definite family resemblance between Jesus'
hymn of jubilation and Mary's Magnificat. As one recognizes in
a child's face certain features of its mother's, so one detects in Jesus'
hymn of jubilation certain traits of Mary's Magnificat. In Nazareth
people said, "The child surely resembles his mother." We say, "Jesus'
prayer reflects as in a mirror that of his mother."

## The Praise of the People of the Covenant

> Blessed be the LORD,
> for he has wondrously shown his
> steadfast love for me (Ps 31:21).

### The Daily Blessings

The piety of the Holy Family was rooted in the pure tradition
of the people of the Covenant.[15] At the heart of this piety, fashioned by the Scriptures, reside blessing and thanksgiving. To the
epiphany of God's love bursting into creation—"the earth is full
of the steadfast love of the LORD," as the psalm sings[16]—to this love
manifested in the history of Israel and in each of our lives—"all
the paths of the LORD are steadfast love and faithfulness," as the
psalm declares[17]—how can humans respond except by welcoming
this tenderness coming down from heaven and by rendering thanks
to God? Better than anyone else, Mary knew that mercy had burst
forth upon the earth. God speaks to human beings by creating
wonders. Human beings respond by blessing the wonder-worker
God. When Tobit opens again his blind eyes on the world's beauty

---

14. Mark 14:36.
15. In this section, we are using again certain elements which we published in
*Célébrer la Parole,* 7 vols. (Paris: Desclée de Brouwer, 1987–1991) 1:76-81.
16. Ps 33:5.
17. Ps 25:10; cf. Tob 3:2.

and discovers the face of fair Sarah, the future mother of his grand-
children, he exclaims:

> Blessed be God,
>    and blessed his great name.[18]

At the same time, he sees the Jerusalem of messianic times rise
on the horizon, the Jerusalem of which it is said:

> The gates of Jerusalem will sing hymns of joy,
>    and all her houses will cry, "Hallelujah!
> Blessed be the God of Israel!"[19]

Of course, it was not people's everyday good fortune to admire a Sarah's beautiful eyes or to hear Jerusalem's streets sing. But
they had reason every morning to bless God for daily benefits. In
Jesus' time, believers lived face-to-face with the Eternal One, in an
unceasing praise of the wonder-worker God. It is this prayer of praise
face-to-face with God that Joseph and Mary revealed to their child.[20]

When they laid him on his mat, they taught him to say, "Blessed
be the One who pours sleep on my eyes and slumber on my eye-
lids." And in the morning upon awakening, "Be praised, you the
Eternal who give life back to the dead." When rising, "Blessed is
He who unfetters the captives." When taking his first steps, "Blessed
be He who directs the steps of humans." When attaching his belt,
"Blessed be He who girds Israel with strength." When washing,
"Grant that today and everyday, I may be a subject of grace, favor,
and mercy in your eyes and in the eyes of those who see me. Be
praised, Eternal, who bestows benefits upon Israel, your people."

Joseph also taught the child the blessing reserved for men, "Be
blessed, Eternal, our God, King of the universe, who did not make
me a woman." One can imagine that Jesus asked Mary, "Imma,
what prayer do *you* say?" And Mary, taking the child in her arms,
answered, "I say, 'Be blessed, Eternal, our God, King of the universe, who created me according to your will.'" Moved with joy,

18. Tob 11:14.
19. Tob 13:17.
20. Readers will find the formulas of blessing in Danby, *The Mishnah*, 1–10, and
M. Schwab, *Le Talmud de Jérusalem*, vol. 1 (Paris: Maisonneuve, 1960), especially
in the Traité des Bénédictions, pp. 215, 403, 487–88. See also R. Aron, *Ainsi priait
Jésus enfant* (Paris: Grasset, 1968). It must be remembered that these blessings are difficult to date but that they perfectly reflect biblical tradition.

she had thought, "Yes, be blessed for having created me a woman. You blessed me among all women. Yes, truly, for me you have done great things; holy is your name."

## The Special Blessings

Besides daily blessings, there were special blessings. When seeing a falling star or flashes of lightning, when enduring storms or tornadoes, people said, "Blessed be the One whose power and strength fill the universe." When glimpsing a rainbow, "Blessed be the One who remembers his Covenant." When admiring the rolling hills, the surging torrents, the blinding light of the desert, "Blessed be the Creator of the universe." When breathing in the fragrances of violets, narcissus, jasmine, "Blessed be the Creator of sweet-scented plants." And when spring set the blossoming trees a-singing, "Praised be the One who does not let the universe lack in anything and who has placed good creatures and beautiful trees for humans to delight in."

It was enjoined to bless God in misfortune as well as in happiness. When happy, people prayed, "Blessed be the Good and Benevolent." And when afflicted, "Blessed be the Judge of truth." When in danger, one was sustained by the trustful prayer of the psalm:

> Blessed be God,
>> because he has not rejected my prayer
>> or removed his steadfast love from me.[21]

Even in the darkest days, like those of the flight into Egypt, the life of the Holy Family was a continual feast of praise and thanksgiving to God. It is inspiring to think that the carpenter from Nazareth and his wife taught their child "to live in thanksgiving" as the Pauline tradition would say later.[22] All his life, Jesus retained this spirit of praise learned in childhood. Indeed, the most characteristic prayer of Jewish piety was the Shemoneh Essreh or the Eighteen Blessings.[23] It was also called Tephillah, that is, "Prayer," because

21. Ps 66:20.
22. Col 3:15 (JB).
23. Readers will find this prayer in a Latin translation in Hänggi-Pahl, *Prex Eucharistica*, pp. 41–44 and in a French translation in Deiss, *Printemps*, 18–23. The relationship between the *Shemoneh Essreh* and the Gospel is set into relief by J. Jeremias

it was the prayer par excellence. As in an immense litany of praise, eighteen blessings form a refrain of thanksgiving and bless God who is beyond all praise. Now, Jesus remembered the Shemoneh Essreh in his hymn of jubilation, quoted above. The beginning of the hymn of jubilation is constructed on the model of the beginning of the Shemoneh Essreh. The earliest redaction, a pre-Christian one, is as follows—with what are regarded as later additions placed in parentheses:

> *You are blessed, Lord our God,*
> (and God of our fathers,
> God of Abraham, God of Isaac, and God of Jacob)
> God great, powerful and redoubtable, God Most High,
> *Lord of heaven and earth,*
> Our shield and the shield of our fathers,
> who increase our trust from generation to generation.
> Blessed are you, Lord, shield of Abraham!

The Shemoneh Essreh is very long. The hymn of jubilation is very short. But precisely, Jesus did not like long formulas. Of course, prayer must be long, even continuous. But not the recitation of prayer formulas. Jesus advised his followers to avoid the use of many words *(polulogia)*, [24] the heaping up of formulas. This is why his hymn is short, like the Our Father. Although brief, the hymn is reminiscent of the prayers learned in the past at his father's and mother's knees.

There were also blessings accompanying meals. When, at the multiplication of the loaves, Luke writes that Jesus took the five loaves, looked up to heaven and blessed them,[25] we must understand that he repeated the formula which Joseph used to recite in Nazareth at the beginning of each meal:

> You are blessed, Lord our God, King of the universe, you who have produced bread from the earth.

It is this same blessing Jesus pronounced at the Last Supper. His way of praying it was so personal that the disciples at Emmaus immediately recognized him "in the breaking of the bread."[26]

---

in his article "La prière quotidienne dans la vie du Seigneur et dans l'Eglise primitive," *La Prière des Heures*, Lex Orandi 35 (1963) 50–51. The Jewish blessings are of prime importance since they are the basis of the Eucharistic prayers of the Christian liturgy.

24. Matt 6:7.
25. Luke 9:16.
26. Luke 24:35.

## The Last Praise

What were, in the midst of his mortal sufferings, the last thoughts of Jesus in agony on the cross? Luke presents Jesus' death in the following way, "Then Jesus, crying with a loud voice, said, 'Father, into your hands I commend my spirit.' Having said this, he breathed his last."[27]

Jesus' last prayer is a quotation from Psalm 31. This psalm is a marvelous summary of Jesus' life, a life made of total trust in the Father.

> Into your hand I commit my spirit. . . .
> But I trust in you, O LORD;
>    I say, "You are my God."
> My times are in your hand.[28]

As his awareness was slowly sinking into the unconsciousness of agony and as his eyes were darkening into death, did Jesus remember the blessing at the end of this psalm, one of the most beautiful praises of God's love?

> Blessed be the LORD,
> for he has wondrously shown his steadfast love to me.[29]

Perhaps then, one last time, his memory evoked the blessed faces of his abba Joseph and his gentle imma at whose knees he had learned, some thirty years before, the ritual formula repeated with tenderness throughout his life, "Be blessed, O Lord."

27. Luke 23:46.
28. Ps 31:5, 14-15.
29. Ps 31:21.

## THE GOD OF MERCY

### God's Mercy According to Mary

In order to bless the Almighty who did wonderful things for her, Mary commemorated God's mercy:

> His mercy [eleos] is for those who fear him
> from generation to generation (Luke 1:50).

> He has helped his servant Israel,
> in remembrance of his mercy [eleos] (Luke 1:54).

With the exception of the word "generation" (in the hackneyed phrase "from generation to generation") which has no religious connotation, the word "mercy" *(eleos)* is the only noun which occurs twice in the Magnificat.[1] Thus, it delimits by an inclusion, as we saw above, the second part of the Magnificat, verses 50 to 55. Mary celebrates God's mercy in the history of Israel, "to Abraham and to his descendants forever."

Mercy was the cradle of her own history. Mercy nurtured the Eternal come down from heaven into her virginal womb. Mercy also transfigured her conjugal love for Joseph whom God had given her as her husband. Mercy was the fountainhead from which her life had sprung and her praise of God drank deep.

Tradition delighted in uniting God and his mercy in one single adoration. Thus, at Sinai, according to Exodus 34:6, God had revealed God's self to Moses as "a God merciful and gracious, slow to anger, and abounding in steadfast love and faithfulness." Now, when this text was read in Hebrew during the service at the synagogue of Nazareth, the Targum rendered it also in Aramaic, "a *merciful* and clement God, patient and inclined to *mercy.*"[2] Similarly, when

---

1. The Synoptics use the word *eleos* ("pity," "mercy," Matt 9:13; 12:7; 23:23; Luke 1:50, 54, 58, 72, 78; 10:37) and the verb *eleein* ("have pity," Matt 5:7; 9:27; 15:22; 17:15; 18:33; 20:30-31; Mark 5:19; 10:47-48; Luke 16:24; 17:13; 18:38-39). Only Luke uses the adjective *oiktirmōn*, which can be translated as "compassionate," "merciful." Mark and John do not use the noun *eleos*. John never uses the verb *eleein*. The Encyclical *Dives in misericordia* (1980) contains a long note (52) on the vocabulary of mercy in the Old Testament. Finally, it must be kept in mind that the way Jesus acted reveals his mercy better than the vocabulary.

2. This translation is that of R. Le Déaut, *Targum du Pentateuque*, 2 vols., Sources chrétiennes 245, 256 (Paris: Cerf, 1978–79) 2:268. The Greek translation of Psalm 103:8

the reading was that of the first account of creation according to Genesis 1:1, "a wind from God swept over the face of the waters," the Targum read, "The spirit of *mercy was sweeping over the waters.*"[3] When meditating on the Holy Spirit that had come upon her and overshadowed her, Mary could rightly think that it was God's mercy that had rested on her. Jesus was the fruit of God's mercy in her womb.

### God's Mercy According to Jesus

This mercy would also rest upon Jesus' soul. Mary's God was assuredly Jesus' God, the God of mercy. When later on Jesus gave his followers the supreme rule of imitating the heavenly Father, he did not first of all invite them to imitate God's holiness. However, he had at his fingertips a formula which even the tiniest child in Israel knew, "You shall be holy, for I the Lord your God am holy."[4] But it is mercy that he gave as a criterion of imitation, as though the holiness of God and the holiness of God's faithful were the holiness of God's mercy:

> Be merciful, just as your Father is merciful.[5]

The people of the Beatitudes whom Jesus summoned into his reign are a merciful people:

> Blessed are the merciful for they will receive mercy.[6]

To the Beatitude of the merciful, Jesus opposed the curse of the scribes and Pharisees who, while tithing mint, dill, and cummin, neglected "the weightier matters of the law: justice and *mercy* and faith."[7]

---

confirms this tradition. It reads, "Compassionate and merciful *[eleēmōn]* is the Lord, long-suffering and rich in mercy *[polueleos]*."

3. See Le Déaut, *Targum du Pentateuque*, 1:75, n. 4.

4. Lev 19:2. See also Lev 11:44-45; 20:26. The formula belongs to the context of the New Testament; it is quoted in 1 Pet 1:16.

5. Luke 6:36. Matt 5:48 has changed the logion to "Be perfect, therefore, as your heavenly Father is perfect." J. Dupont, *Les Béatitudes*, 3 vols., Etudes Bibliques (Paris: Gabalda, 1969-73) 3:325, notes, "It is obvious that Matthew wanted to widen the perspective."

6. Matt 5:7.

7. Matt 23:23; Luke 11:42. The Gospels report several logia which present the Pharisees in a very unfavorable light. Let us make clear once for all that these nega-

To firmly impress the duty of mercy on his listeners' memory, Jesus invented the parable of the two debtors. Both are insolvent. One, who is in debt to their "lord" (let us understand, "God"), obtains the remission of his debt. But he is condemned afterwards for not having had mercy, as he received mercy, on his fellow servant who is in debt to him. In the parable, the lord states Jesus' rule as follows, "Should you not have *had mercy* on your fellow slave, as I *had mercy* on you?"[8]

The very ministry of Jesus appeared as the face of God's mercy on earth. The long procession that accompanied Jesus step by step and entreated his pity—the father, so humble in his faith, who implored the healing of his child; the Canaanite woman, so bold, who asked for some crumbs fallen from the children's table; the ten lepers among whom was the thankful Samaritan; the blind Bartimaeus, who leapt for joy before Jesus—all these beggars for Jesus' love, in their various afflictions appealed to Jesus' pity, "Jesus—or Lord, Master, Son of David—*have mercy*."[9]

The scribes and the Pharisees, who passed themselves off as the official interpreters of the Law, deemed that Jesus' kindness overstepped the limits their wisdom had imposed on God's mercy. When Jesus called Matthew, the tax collector, to follow him, they did not dare confront Jesus himself for fear of losing face; but they questioned his disciples, "Why does your teacher eat with tax collectors and sinners?" Jesus overheard the question and, quoting the prophet Hosea, retorted:

---

tive judgments do not apply in any way to pious Pharisees who were seeking God's reign, such as the Pharisee Nicodemus (John 3:1), but only to teachers who falsified God's word by their hypocrisy (see Matt 23:13-33, "Woe to you, scribes and Pharisees, hypocrites"). On the other hand, certain logia attributed to Jesus reflect in fact the opposition around the years 70–80 of certain Jewish circles to the young Christian Church which had broken with the Synagogue. The same must be said of the expression "the Jews," which occurs five times in Matthew, but seventy-one times in John, very often with an unfavorable connotation and sometimes identifying them with the Pharisees. See F. Mussner, *Traité sur les Juifs*, Cogitatio fidei 109 (Paris: Cerf, 1981) 303. Jesus' religious practice, in general, was that of devout Pharisaism.

8. Matt 18:33. Matthew has placed this parable at the end of the "church order" discourse (ch. 18) to underline the importance of mutual compassion and forgiveness in the Christian community.

9. Here are the references: the father of the epileptic boy, Matt 17:15; the Canaanite woman, Matt 15:22; the ten lepers, Luke 17:13; Bartimaeus, Mark 10:47-48; Matt 20:31-32 (Matt 9:27 is probably a doublet); Luke 18:38-39. To be complete, one should add the parable of the good Samaritan, who is given as an example: he had pity on his neighbor (Luke 10:33) and he practiced mercy (10:37).

Go and learn what this means, "I desire mercy, not sacrifice."[10]

By exercising his ministry of mercy, Jesus therefore accomplished the will of the God of mercy.

### "Tell Them How Much the Lord Has Done for You"

One of the most moving cures is that of the Gerasene demoniac. After healing this man with an unclean spirit, Jesus got back into the boat in order to cross to the other side of the lake. The cured man was begging him to be allowed to remain with him. Jesus refused his request but said to him:

> Go home to your friends, and tell them how much the Lord has done for you, and what *mercy* he has shown you.[11]

If Mary knew of this episode, and especially of this wondrous ending—Mark is the only one who has recorded it—she must have loved it a great deal. Jesus linked in one single proclamation the wonder God worked for the cured man and the praise of God's mercy. Is there not here something like a memory of the Magnificat?

Like all mothers, Mary left her imprint on the memory and heart of her child. And this influence on the little boy of the humble Galilean woman, in the house of Joseph the carpenter of Nazareth, later marked the preaching of the Rabbi Yeshua Ben Yoseph and in the end changed the face of the earth. Can we not picture Mary, her bare feet in her sandals, hugging the child in the folds of her robe and whispering to him, "Tinoki, my little one, listen carefully to me. God's mercy extends from age to age on those who fear God.[12] God's mercy reaches to your father; God's mercy reaches to me, your mother. And God's mercy reaches to you, my child. During all of your life imitate God's mercy. And proclaim it."

This is exactly what Jesus did later on.

10. Matt 9:9-13. Jesus quotes Hos 6:6.
11. Mark 5:19.
12. Luke 1:49-50.

# THE GOD OF THE POOR

He has filled the hungry with good things
and sent the rich away empty (Luke 1:53).

## The Magnificat, Song of the Poor

In an image filled with tenderness, Psalm 109:31 declares that God "stands at the right hand of the needy." Mary's song is the praise which the needy offer to the God of the Covenant who stands at their right. The Hebrew Bible calls them the *anawim*. They are the weak, the persecuted, the unfortunate, the poor, the widows and orphans. . . . They are the immense family of God's beggars, the friends of God's love. "The poor have become God's relatives. Poverty expresses a power to welcome God, an openness toward God, an availability to God, a humility before God."[1]

Hannah, Samuel's mother, had foreshadowed Mary's praise when she sang the God of the poor in these words:

The LORD makes poor and makes rich;
    he brings low, he also exalts.
He raises up the poor from the dust;
    he lifts the needy from the ash heap.[2]

By stating that God fills the hungry with good things but sends the rich away empty-handed, Mary was in complete agreement with the tradition of Israel. Anyway, she was placing herself, along with Joseph, among that endless procession of the poor since they lived together in real poverty. When they presented the child in the Temple, they offered "a pair of turtledoves or two young pigeons," which was the sacrifice of the poor.[3]

This experience of poverty marked Jesus' consciousness. Mary's song of poverty was the spiritual environment in which the great themes of the gospel symphony would be born. The very first homily of Jesus in Nazareth, according to Luke's tradition, begins with the

1. A. Gelin, *Les Pauvres de Yahvé* (Paris: Cerf, 1953) 29.
2. 1 Sam 2:7-8.
3. Luke 2:24. See Lev 5:7 and 12:8. It is interesting to note that, according to Hegesippus, after the Lord's resurrection, Jesus' family continued to hold on to the tradition of poverty (Eusebius of Caesarea, *Histoire Ecclésiastique*, III, 20:1-6, Sources Chrétiennes 31 [Paris: Cerf, 1952] 123–24).

affirmation that his messianic ministry is addressed primarily to the poor.

> The Spirit of the Lord is upon me,
> because he has anointed me
> to bring good news to the poor.[4]

Luke's tradition is confirmed by Matthew's. In the Sermon on the Mount, which is the first of the five great discourses of Matthew's tradition, Jesus establishes the Church of the Beatitudes, that is, of those who are proclaimed blessed according to God's judgment. Now, the first of the Beatitudes, which opens the entrance to this community, is that of the poor:

> Blessed are the poor in spirit,
> for theirs is the kingdom of heaven.[5]

At home in Nazareth, they still said, "God sends the rich away empty." Later on, Jesus remembered his mother's song of poverty when he proclaimed in his initial discourse according to Luke's tradition:

> Blessed are you who are poor,
> for yours is the kingdom of God. . . .
> But woe to you who are rich,
> for you have received your consolation.[6]

Due to catechetical concern, Matthew adds that what is meant here is (also) poverty "in spirit," therefore a spiritual disposition, for material poverty is blessed only if it opens the heart to God's riches. But Mary of Nazareth and Jesus of the Beatitudes speak of a universal poverty and so include the sort of material poverty that was experienced in the everyday life of Nazareth.

Mary also said:

> He has filled the hungry *[peinōntas]* with good things.[7]

Jesus remembered the hungry his mother was speaking about. He declared in his first discourse according to Luke:

---

4. Luke 4:18.

5. Matt 5:3.

6. Luke 1:53; 6:20, 24. The curses, which only Luke presents, "appear not to belong to the context [of the Beatitudes], and the hypothesis of an addition by Luke is quite likely." M.-E. Boismard, *Synopse des quatre Evangiles*, vol. 2 (Paris: Cerf, 1972) 127.

7. Luke 1:53.

Blessed are you who are hungry *[peinōntas]* now,
   for you will be filled. . . .
Woe to you who are full now,
   for you will be hungry.[8]

Here again, Matthew, out of catechetical concern, stresses that what is meant is (also) those who hunger and thirst for righteousness. But Mary in her Magnificat and Jesus in the Beatitudes thought of real bodily hunger, the hunger people asked God to satisfy when they said, "give us today our daily bread."

All through his messianic ministry, Jesus lived in poverty. When he sent his disciples on their mission during the Galilean[9] period, he commanded them to take no gold or silver or copper, or bag, or a change of tunics, or sandals, or a staff. . . . What is discussed here is probably not a set of fastidious rulings, but rather the spirit of the mission: the announcement of the reign cannot allow itself to be entangled in worries about possessions. Living without personal resources, unable to support himself when he was preaching the good news, Jesus had accepted, in plain view of everyone, material help from a group of women who gave him alms.[10] His poverty was luminous, without ostentation or dissimulation. He readily accepted invitations to dinner, even those of wealthy persons, such as Zacchaeus, a tax collector, who the gospel expressly says was rich.[11] Only once did he let slip a melancholy remark concerning his itinerant and solitary condition:

Foxes have holes, and birds of the air have nests; but the Son of Man has nowhere to lay his head.[12]

Some Pharisees, described as lovers of money and devourers of widows' houses, had mocked him for declaring that one cannot serve God and mammon. He shot back, "What is prized by human beings is an abomination in the sight of God."[13] There is an irreducible opposition between the grace of the gospel and the love of money.

8. Luke 6:21, 25. Cf. Matt 5:6.
9. Mission of the Twelve, Matt 10:9-13; Mark 6:8-10; Luke 9:3-4. Mission of the seventy-two: Luke 10:4-5 (the text is probably a doublet of 9:3-4).
10. Luke 8:1-3.
11. Luke 19:2.
12. Matt 8:20; Luke 9:58.
13. Luke 16:13-15; 20:47; Mark 12:40.

## Like Mother, Like Son

At times, the Magnificat has been presented as a warlike, even revolutionary song. One must understand this correctly: here it is a question of revolution according to God, the revolution which overcomes hatred with love, pride with humility. Nevertheless, it is true that certain statements of the Magnificat express a singular violence. They also lack theological precision. "He has brought down the powerful from their thrones," said Mary. She should have added, "not all the powerful; only those who are vicious and domineering." For it is possible to be powerful and kind. She also asserted, "[He has] sent the rich away empty." She should have specified, "the evil rich." To be rich does not make one unfit for the reign of God, but to misuse one's riches does. Similarly, it is not a grace in God's eyes simply to be humble—there were in ancient times many philosophers who lived in humility; there are today many "pagans" who live in intelligent humility—but it is a grace to remain humble before God because of the reign.[14] Therefore, there is in Mary a certain lack of nuance. Would she be only a theologian of small stature? Besides, one notes in her a tendency to exaggeration, which is a characteristic of popular speech. Let us say however that there is nothing to worry about concerning Mary's theology. A perceptive and intelligent woman, she amiably supposes that we too are perceptive and intelligent, that, aided by our Christian common sense, we understand rightly what she means.

It is exactly Mary's way of thinking—and theologizing—that we find in Jesus.

Matthew's Jesus says, "Blessed are the poor in spirit." But Luke's Jesus simply says, without any qualification, as Mary would have said, "Blessed are you who are poor." And this was the way the Beatitude was originally enunciated. Matthew's Jesus also says, "Blessed are those who hunger and thirst for righteousness." But Luke's Jesus says, "Blessed are you who are hungry now." And this is the original form of the Beatitude.[15] Clearly, the Beatitudes resemble the Magnificat. Jesus resembles his mother.[16]

14. See Matt 5:46-48.
15. See Dupont, *Béatitudes*, 1:212-23.
16. M.-J. Lagrange, *Evangile selon Luc*, 54, notes, "She [Mary] understood God's kindness to the little ones and God's compassion for the poor. These would be Jesus' feelings."

Jesus also appears as a master of oriental hyperbole. He excelled in finding dazzling images that hooked the hearers' attention and imprinted themselves in their memory. Thus he censured some Pharisees' duplicity by calling them camel-swallowers and gnat-strainers,[17] words that the people must have gleefully drunk in. He also asked whether one gathers grapes from thorns or figs from thistles, and added, "A good tree cannot bear bad fruit, nor can a bad tree bear good fruit."[18] Which is obviously untrue, for it is possible for a good tree to occasionally bear some bad fruit. But this is perfectly applicable to the orchards in the parables imagined by Jesus, in which precisely we learn to recognize by their fruit false prophets and prophets according to God's heart.

He also declared that it is easier for a camel to go through the eye of a needle than for someone who is rich to enter the reign of God.[19] Which is obviously exaggerated. It is even contrary to the gospel since Jesus counted among his disciples wealthy persons open to the gospel, all candidates for the reign, such as Joseph of Arimathea, who is expressly said to have been rich[20] and to have given his new tomb as the burial place for Jesus' body.

He also taught that one must not resist evil people, which is in accordance with his gospel of love. But why did he add that one must offer the left cheek to the person who slapped the right? He himself did not do so. When he was before Caiaphas and one of the police struck him, he reacted with vigor, "If I have spoken wrongly, testify to the wrong. But if I have spoken rightly, why do you strike me?"[21]

Was there a theological intention behind Jesus' hyperbolic language? Undoubtedly.[22] In his flamboyant images and his stunning comparisons, Jesus expressed according to his charism of popular preacher, the radical nature of the gospel, the absolute necessity of conversion. He could have been content with saying, "It will be

17. Matt 23:24.
18. See Matt 7:15-18; 12:33; Luke 6:43-44.
19. Matt 19:24; Mark 10:25; Luke 18:25.
20. Matt 27:57.
21. Matt 5:39; Luke 6:29; John 18:23.
22. M. Gourgues, "Prier les Hymnes du Nouveau Testament," *Cahiers Evangile* 80 (Paris: Cerf) 40, perceptively remarks, "For instance, in Matthew, the Beatitude of the poor emphasizes the disposition of believers (the 'poor in spirit') with regard to God (5:3); in Luke, it emphasizes those of God with regard to believers (6:20)." Also, pages 35–43 concerning the Magnificat are excellent.

hard for rich people to enter the kingdom of heaven," and adding, "if they are not converted." But instead of giving this liberating specification, he reinforces the difficulty with the hyperbole of the camel having to go through the eye of a needle. Here, it is no longer difficulty, but impossibility. In the same way, Mary could have said, "It is so difficult for rich people with full hands to welcome the reign—"if they do not get converted," being understood—"that God sends them away empty-handed." And, "It is so difficult for powerful people to be humble"—"if they do not get converted," being understood—"that God brings them down from their thrones."

But Jesus also stressed God's power. When the disciples anxiously asked, "Then who can be saved?" he answered, "For mortals it is impossible, but for God all things are possible."[23]

This notion of God's saving power must have been long familiar to Jesus. When Sadducees began a discussion on the resurrection and thought they would embarrass him by inventing the story of the woman with the seven husbands, Jesus responded by invoking God's power, "Is not this the reason you are wrong, that you know neither the scriptures nor the power of God?"[24] It is as if he were saying, "God is more powerful than your scholarly debates may suppose. God of the living, God creates the world of the resurrection; the power of God's love makes the risen ones like angels."[25]

This theme of God's power was like daily bread at Nazareth. The word "for God all things are *possible*" resembles like a twin Gabriel's word "nothing will be *impossible* with God."[26] When Mary sang that the *Mighty One* had done great things for her, she remembered full well that the *power* of the *Most High* had overshadowed her[27] and caused the divine infant to be conceived in her virginal womb. Was it not for her the supreme manifestation of the power of God, who masters the impossible?

How rightly people say, "Like mother, like son." Like Mary, like Jesus.

23. Matt 19:25-26; see Mark 10:26-27; Luke 18:26-27.
24. Mark 12:24.
25. Matt 22:30; Mark 12:25; Luke 20:36.
26. Luke 1:37.
27. Luke 1:34.

# THE GOD OF THE HUMBLE

He has looked with favor on the lowliness of his servant. (Luke 1:48)

Akin to the theme of poverty is that of humility. The God who saves the poor is also the God who loves the humble.

This certitude is part and parcel of what could be called the religious heritage of humankind. During their sojourn in Egypt, the people of Abraham lived in the religious environment of Egyptian wisdom. In Egypt, people knew that God heard the prayer of the humble. The blind scribe Pawah addresses to the god Amon this admirable prayer:

> My heart desires to see you,
> my heart is full of joy, Amon, protector of the poor!
> You are the father of the motherless,
> the husband of the widow. . . .
> Incline [toward me] your beauteous face.
> You will come from afar!
> Grant that your humble servant, the scribe Pawah, may see you.[1]

The sages of Israel collected in their own tradition similar prayers and transcribed them into the Psalter: "He leads the humble in what is right, / and teaches the humble his way."[2] "For though the LORD is high, he regards the lowly; / but the haughty he perceives from far away."[3] Sovereign judge, God rises "to save all the oppressed of the earth."[4] Judith summarizes the religious experience of Israel when she invokes the God of victories as the God who saves the humble:

> But you are the God of the lowly, helper of the oppressed, upholder of the weak, protector of the forsaken, savior of those without hope.[5]

---

1. *Hymnes et Prières de l'Egypte Ancienne,* Littératures anciennes du Proche-Orient (Paris: Cerf, 1980) 204–5. This prayer probably goes back to the Amarna period, that is, to the fourteenth century B.C.E.
2. Ps 25:9.
3. Ps 138:6.
4. Ps 76:9. See also Ps 10:18; 18:27; 34:2; 37:11; 69:33; 147:6; 149:4.
5. Jdt 9:11.

## Mary, the Humble Servant

Mary naturally fitted in among the humble of Israel. In the Magnificat, she spoke both of humility and the humble:

> He has looked with favor on the *lowliness [tapeinōsin]*
> of his servant (Luke 1:48).
> He has brought down the powerful from their thrones,
> and lifted up the lowly *[tapeinous]* (Luke 1:52).

The noun *tapeinōsis* can be translated by both "humiliation" and "humility." When Hannah, in the sanctuary at Shiloh, begged the Lord to look upon her *tapeinōsis and give her "a male child,"*[6] and thus anticipated Mary's Magnificat, she of course was thinking of the humiliation inflicted by her rival Peninnah's mocking remarks: Hannah was the preferred wife but was childless, whereas Peninnah had children. When Mary spoke of her *tapeinōsis*, she was obviously thinking of her lowliness, that is, her humble condition as a daughter of Israel on whom God had looked with favor.

Theoretically, what counts on the religious plane is not humiliation but humility. Not humiliation before human beings, but humility before God. But in fact, God's tenderness is so universal that God takes care of both the humiliated and the humble, of Hannah's humiliation and Mary's humility. Both belong to the immense throng of the *anawim.*

## Jesus, Humble of Heart

Jesus followed in Mary's footsteps. He seems to have quoted a word of the Magnificat when he declared:

> All who exalt themselves will be humbled, and all who humble themselves will be exalted.

We have here a "traveling logion," that is, a saying that may be used as the conclusion to different stories. This means it was familiar to Jesus' way of thinking and he may have quoted it repeatedly as a universal principle. Thus, the logion is in Luke as the conclusion to the parable dealing with the choice of places and the

6. LXX 1 Sam 1:11.

parable of the Pharisee and the tax collector.[7] Matthew inserts it, with a minimal change, in the discourse against some Pharisees.[8] The passive voice, "will be humbled," "will be exalted," is the "divine passive." We must understand, "God will humble," "God will exalt." It is probable that the logion originally had an eschatological connotation:[9] "Those who exalt themselves will be humbled by God on the last day, and those who humble themselves will be exalted by God on the last day." As is his custom, Luke gives such sayings a moralizing tone. Then, the logion appears no longer as a criterion of the last judgment but as a rule of conduct for the time of the Church. We may certainly think it was in the workshop in Nazareth, in the place where Jesus was learning his religion, that the saying was coined and imprinted on the memory of the child.

To this theme, an exquisite Marian note is to be added. Mary declared that the Lord had scattered "the proud in the thoughts of their hearts" or, to translate absolutely verbatim, "those who were proud by the thought of their hearts."[10] At his home in Nazareth, they did not like proud hearts, those who boasted before Yahweh. They preferred those who said with a childlike simplicity, as in Psalm 131, "O Lord, my heart is not lifted up, / my eyes are not raised too high." They affirmed that God scattered proud hearts and looked down with love on humble hearts. Later on, when Jesus invited his disciples to imitate him, he gave them as a model the humility of his heart, "Learn from me; for I am gentle and humble in heart."[11] Jesus' gentle and humble heart[12] stands in contrast to the proud hearts Mary disapproved of. The proud hearts, God scatters. The gentle and humble hearts, Jesus gathered to make his disciples. Obviously, Jesus' religion was, like Mary's, the religion of humility of heart.

---

7. Luke 14:7-11; 18:9-14.

8. Matt 23:12.

9. J. Jeremias, *Les paraboles de Jésus* (Paris: Mappus, 1962) 184–85.

10. Luke 1:51. The translation used in the Lectionary and the Liturgy of the Hours simply says, "he has confused the proud in their inmost thoughts." The word *heart* has been left out. Therefore, no allusion to Jesus' heart is suggested. Anyhow, it is true that the liturgical translation has often chosen to favor an idea and eliminate a biblical image. Another case is the translation of Eph 1:18 which has removed the biblical image of "the eyes of [the] heart" which are enlightened; the Lectionary says "innermost vision."

11. Matt 11:29.

12. According to C. Spicq, *Notes de Lexicographie Néo-Testamentaire* (Göttingen: Vandenhoeck & Ruprecht, 1978) 879, "Christian humility . . . unites the notions of poverty, modesty, gentleness."

Together in Nazareth, Mary and Jesus could read in the Book
of Isaiah the story of their lives:

> Thus says the LORD:
> Heaven is my throne
>   and the earth is my footstool; . . .
> But this is the one to whom I will look,
>   to the humble and contrite in spirit,
>   who trembles at my word.[13]

## The Annunciation, Feast of Humility

A "servant" is about to conceive "the Son of the Most High";
time is about to welcome eternity; the lowliness of human nature
is about to open to the infinite mercy of God: such is the Annunciation, feast of humility.

Forget the one thousand and one representations of the
annunciation—certain paintings are sublime masterpieces—in which
we see Mary dressed as a princess, wrapped in a robe sparkling with
gold stars, crowned with a halo of glory, and Gabriel scintillating
with flaming wings in a whirlwind of light. Think, rather, not of a
royal mansion made of polished stone, but of a Galilean cob-walled
house, one of those earthen houses whose walls, Jesus said, could
be broken through:[14] this is the setting where the story of Jesus
began—Jesus, the Savior of the world, the King of ages, the Lord
of eternities—and God entered into conversation with a young girl
of thirteen or fourteen. What a reversal of order in a society dominated by men, in which it was said even in Christian liturgies, "As
in all the churches of the saints, women should be silent in the
churches."[15] They were to be silent in the assemblies, but they talked
with God concerning the salvation of the world. They had no place
in the liturgical celebrations; they were simply asked to remain submissive to men and to wear a veil on their heads as a sign of that

13. Isa 66:1-2. The text of the Septuagint uses *tapeinos* ("humble") and *ēsuchios*
("calm," "peaceful"): "the humble and peaceful who revere my word."
14. Matt 6:19.
15. 1 Cor 14:33-34. Nowadays, this text is regarded as an interpolation. But the
spirit of this interpolation is still sometimes present in the Church. See the remarks
of J.-A. Aubert, "Dichotomie sexuelle, antiféminisme et structures d'Eglise," *Le Supplément* 161 (1987) 53-62.

submission, "because of the angels";[16] and here was Gabriel assuring Mary she was full of grace, filled with God's love and beauty. What an exaltation of the humble, what an overthrow of the powerful from their thrones of pride in a religion dominated by lawyers, teachers of the Law, and priests! They thought they knew everything about God and the world, and here was God addressing a young girl, asking her to accept, as a free human being, to work along with God. And the lowly Galilean became the mother of the Eternal One.

16. According to 1 Cor 11:10, which is difficult to interpret. Perhaps the angels were supposed to see to the good order of the assemblies. Or does the word "angels" replace the word "God"?

## MARY AND JESUS, SERVANTS

Twice, Mary calls herself the servant *doulē* of the Lord. The first time is in the conversation of the Annunciation, "Here am I, the servant of the Lord; let it be with me according to your word" (Luke 1:38). The second time is in the Magnificat, "He has looked with favor on the lowliness of his servant *[doulē]*" (1:48). In what we could call "Mary's religion," this title is at the heart of her vocation. Indeed, her divine motherhood is rooted in the humility of this title.

### Vocabulary: The Meaning of *doulos* and *doulē*

It is important to specify the meaning of *doulos, doulē* ("male servant," "female servant") in biblical vocabulary.

### *Slave*

In its strict sense, the Greek *doulos,* like its Hebrew equivalent *ebed,* means "slave." In pagan antiquity, slaves had no personal freedom, and therefore lived in total dependency on their owners. The latter had bought them with money or had inherited them and could use them as they pleased, even sexually[1]; they could resell them at their whim. A funerary inscription going back to the time of Tiberius (d. 37)—and so contemporary with Jesus—betrays all the distress of the slave: "Here I lie buried, I, Lemiso. Only death put an end to my labors."[2]

Israel knew about slavery on foreign soil and even had the personal experience of it. We recall that Joseph was sold into slavery by his brothers for twenty pieces of silver—which in ancient Babylonia was the price of an ox[3]—and taken to Egypt, "the house of slavery."[4]

1. P. Kieffer and L. Rydbeck, *Existence païenne au début du Christianisme* (Paris; Cerf, 1983) 18–19.
2. Ibid., 19. The inscription is written in popular Latin: *Heic situs sum Lemiso, quem numquam nisi mors feinivit labore.*
3. De Vaux, *Institutions,* 1:131.
4. Exod 13:3.

*Servants in the Land of Israel*

Imitating pagan nations, the people of God accepted the social evil of slavery, although they humanized it somewhat. Slaves became *servants* in their owner's house. Male servants were circumcised and therefore integrated into the Covenant, rested on the Sabbath—theoretically, there was no Lemiso in the land of Israel—participated in certain prayers, and celebrated certain religious feasts, particularly Passover, with their master's family. There was even a current saying in Jerusalem, "Is your daughter of age? Free your slave and give her to him in marriage."[5] Finally, slaves were supposed to be freed in the seventh year.[6] Female servants became the maids of the mistress or the nurses of her children. They could also be the concubines of the master or the master's son.[7]

*Child and Son*

In certain cases, the Hebrew *ebed* and the Greek *doulos* can be rendered by *pais* ("child"), which can also be understood as *huios* ("son").[8] This fluidity of vocabulary is found equally in the Gospels. Thus, in the story of the cure of the centurion's servant in Capernaum, this servant is called *child* in Matthew 8:6, *servant* in Luke 7:3, and *son* in John 4:47. In fact, the flexibility of the vocabulary attests to the diversity of the situations in which slaves found themselves and also the diversity of their owners' characters.

**Mary, Servant of the Lord**

But when the master is God and is revealed as infinite Love, then the slave enters a slavery of love, which is at the same time the most sublime liberation. The title of servant of the Lord becomes

5. Deut 15:12-18.

6. The law code of Hammurabi forbade the selling of a female slave who had children in her master's house. This may be found in the sixth volume of the collection *Littératures anciennes du Proche-Orient* 6 (Paris: Cerf, 1983) 90–91.

7. Jeremias, *Paraboles*, 160–61. The saying recalls the case mentioned in 1 Chr 2:34-35.

8. Thus, in the second Song of the Servant of Yahweh, Isa 49:1-6, the Septuagint renders the Hebrew *ebed* by either *doulos* ("slave," vv. 3, 5) or *pais* ("child," v. 6). P. Grelot notes that "in fact, the two terms are equivalent in the Septuagint translation of Isaiah." *Les poèmes du Serviteur*, Lectio Divina 103 (Paris: Cerf, 1981) 90.

the title of the highest nobility. Such was Mary's slavery—slave, servant, and daughter of God.

*Slave of God*, captured by God's love, Mary placed her freedom completely in her Master's hands.

*Servant of the Lord*, she belonged to God's household. Inasmuch as she is Jesus' mother, she is at the head of the servants. The best servant. And the best loved.

The Letter to the Ephesians (2:19) declares in a felicitous phrase that the faithful are members of the "household" *(oikeioi)* of God, that they are fellow-citizens of the saints of heaven, that is, from the same city *(sumpolitai)* as the saints. It could be said that Mary was from the same village as Abraham. For the same word which was spoken in former times near Sarah's tent in Mamre had been heard also in the village of Nazareth, "For nothing is impossible with God."[9] Mary placed herself in Abraham's family. The mercy formerly promised "to Abraham and his descendants forever"[10] had now reached as far as the home in Nazareth and from there spread to the entire universe.

*Child, daughter of God*, Mary walks at the head of all the sons and daughters of God. As daughter of Zion,[11] she is the most pure and intense personification of this Israel which, in his prayer for the restoration of the chosen people, Sirach called "Israel . . . your firstborn."[12]

## Mary's Obedience

### At the Heart of Obedience

The vocation of Mary, the servant, found its unity in her maternity. One could also say that this maternity was the source of all the other marvels which flourished in the garden of her heart. Her obedience to this vocation, that is, to become Jesus' mother, represented the summit of her submission as a servant.

---

9. Gen 18:14; Luke 1:37.
10. Luke 1:55.
11. Dogmatic Constitution on the Church, *Lumen Gentium*, no. 55. See Deiss, *Marie, fille de Sion* (Paris: Desclée de Brouwer, 1959) 12. (*Mary, Daughter of Sion*, trans. Barbara T. Blair [Collegeville, Minn.: The Liturgical Press, 1972].)
12. Sir 36:17.

Having so often read the story of the Annunciation with all we know of the events that are going to happen from Bethlehem to the first Pentecost, having in our memory the stamp of twenty centuries of Christianity, we perhaps forget too often that Mary's situation had something absolutely stupefying and unique; there has been nothing like it since the creation of the world, since a man and a woman were created to live together and love one another. Here was a young girl engaged to Joseph the carpenter and therefore, according to the laws of the time,[13] in the position of a bride not yet living with her husband. And the angel Gabriel suddenly burst into her house and told her she was to become pregnant with a child from heaven.

Of course, the angel enumerated the titles of this marvelous child: he would be great, he would be called Son of the Most High, he would possess the throne of his father David, his reign would have no end. But all these titles were in the future and belonged to the domain of prophecy. Now, as everyone knows, there is a world, sometimes as big as an abyss, between prophecy and its fulfillment. Thus, when the prophet Nathan, in what is called the charter of the house of David,[14] announced to David that God would be like a father to him and he would be like a son to God; that his house, his kingship, and his throne would be made firm for eternity, David could not have guessed that the earthly kingship of his dynasty would end in the rags and tatters and sobbing of the deportation to Babylon; that his house would be only a "fallen . . . hut."[15] He could not have known that, despite all this, on the horizon of history, a child would be born, Jesus, who would build for him an eternal reign in heaven, and that this child would be the only son of God, would lead not only David's people, but the whole of humankind to the shores of God's eternity. Likewise, when the angel promised Mary that her child would be called son of God and his reign would have no end, Mary could not have suspected that one day he would be nailed to a cross and then rise in the glory of the only Son of God.

At the time of the Annunciation, Mary was alone. There was only a young Galilean woman face to face with an angel bringing

13. See pp. 25–29.
14. 2 Sam 7:5-15.
15. Amos 9:11.

her promises of eternity whose infinite depth she could not imagine—and an absent husband. The only certitude was that God had intervened in her life. Her only response was an unconditional leap into God's mystery. And a very simple obedience, "let it be with me according to your word."

### *"How Can This Be?"*

Throughout the narrative, Mary appears as a young woman perfectly calm, poised, full of common sense. Not a trace of emotional exaltation. To the angel's announcement, she responds with a question, "How can this be, since I am a virgin?"[16]

The Greek says, "I do not know a man," and "know" is a euphemism to designate sexual relations. Now, Mary was engaged to a *man*, Joseph. She could therefore know him. How then does she say that she does not know a *man*? How are we to understand her question? Does it still have any meaning? If so, what meaning?

Mary's word has often been interpreted as, if not a vow, at least a resolution of virginity. Mary would have declared that she did not know a man to signify a state in which she had decided to remain. This is the most common explanation. In the past, it allowed ascetical circles to exalt the value of virginity because Mary had chosen it. But in our opinion such an explanation does not withstand analysis of the text.

Such a resolution of virginity on Mary's part would have manifested an autonomy which young girls of her time did not have. In Israel, as is still true in certain countries of the Middle East and elsewhere, a young girl did not freely dispose of herself but was always under the authority of a man, either her father if she was still unmarried or her husband if she was married. In any case, it was her father who married her, that is, gave her in marriage to a husband. Scripture advised, "Give a daughter in marriage, / and you complete a great task."[17]

And above all, if Mary's father gave her in marriage to Joseph, it was in the hope she would insure he had a descendant. No father gives his daughter in marriage in the hope that she will remain childless. And nowhere in the world does one get engaged to remain

16. Luke 1:34.
17. Sir 7:25.

a virgin. Nowhere in the world—still less in the land of Israel at that time—does one get married in order to renounce the joys of love and children.

We must come back to Luke's text, read it as simply as possible, place it back within the spiritual environment of the time. "A virginal conception, that is, a conception that would happen in a purely supernatural way, without the man's participation, was for the Old Testament impossible to imagine."[18] The history of Israel knew of marvelous births to barren women—such as Sarah, Rebekah, and Rachel, the wives of Abraham, Isaac, and Jacob—but not of a virginal conception. "Even in Mary's time, people thought of a purely human conception and birth of the Messiah."[19] Mary is the daughter of her tradition; Scripture is her home. The angel tells her to conceive her child at once. Therefore she asks how this can be done right now since, she says, she does "not know" (*ou gignoskō*, in the present tense) a man. How can she become a mother at that very moment as all mothers become mothers, by union with their husbands, since she does not yet live with her husband?

This most obvious explanation[20] fully respects the tradition in which Mary lived. It gives Luke's text a perfectly coherent meaning. Above all, it reveals that the essential thing for Mary is neither to live in virginity nor to live in celibacy nor to live in marriage, but quite simply to accomplish God's will: she is God's servant. More than virginity, more than marriage, more even than motherhood, what constitutes the summit of Mary's religion is this total obedience to God's will. There is only one absolute in Mary's life: God's will. This is the absolute of love.

### The Obedience of Faith

When we reread the story of the Annunciation with eyes that are capable of wonderment, it seems that we hear a two-voice choir

---

18. D. Haugg, *Das erste biblische Marien Wort* (Stuttgart: Verlag Kath. Bibelwerk, 1938) 64.

19. Ibid., 71.

20. Cajetan (1480–1547) proposed this long ago; it is mentioned by Lagrange, *Evangile selon Luc*, 32. It was taken up in the excellent study of Haugg, *Marien Wort*, pp. 61–73, and more recently by Grelot, *Les poèmes*, 217–18, and George, *Etudes sur Luc*, 436–37. We ourselves have analyzed the text of the Annunciation in *Célébrer la Parole* (1987) 4:51-62.

of sublime beauty, one in which melodies are interconnected in the blazing of flaming harmonies. . . . There is the high voice, that of heaven, that of Gabriel. It announces the messianic joy to the one who is full of grace, the presence of Emmanuel in her womb, Jesus' divine filiation, the triumph of his eternal reign. We also hear the humble voice of Mary, full of womanly beauty. Gabriel's words could have dazzled her. What young woman was ever hailed as wondrously? But Mary retains an immovable simplicity. This announcement touches her at the most intimate depths of her flesh, at the very heart of her femininity, for this whole story will find its culmination in what happened in her womb. She remains wholly woman, a very practical woman, with her two feet on the ground, as if to say, "Dear angel, let's talk sensibly: my fiancé, Joseph, isn't here; I don't live in his house yet. Just how is this conception to come about?" Is this not a stunning candor?

The angel speaks again in the language of heaven:

> The holy Spirit will come upon you, and the power of the Most High will overshadow you.

At least, such is what we read in Luke 1:35, according to the translation commonly offered. Even if this "dialogue" with Gabriel were only a spiritual understanding of what God was asking of her, even if, similarly, her answer were only the inner consent of her will, it remains that Luke's words best express this mystery. Or, if we restore to Luke's words their archaic flavor, Mary could understand:

> Holy breath (spirit) will come upon you and power of the most High will take you in its shadow.[21]

To speak plainly, "the holy breath of God—breath that awakens life—and the power of the Most High—the God of the impossible—will fulfill this conception in you." Only later on, after Jesus' resurrection, would the community be able to understand that the *Holy Breath* of the story of the annunciation was in fact the *Holy Spirit*, the gift of the Father.

---

21. We observe that Luke loves to associate the concepts of spirit and power. Thus, he states that John the Baptist would walk "with the spirit and power of Elijah" (1:17) and that Jesus was anointed "with the Holy Spirit and with power" (Acts 10:38).

For Mary, as for each of us, the principle is valid, "We walk by faith, not by sight."[22] Mary did not always have a clear view of her own vocation, still less of its ineffable splendor. She is perplexed by Gabriel's salutation;[23] she is amazed by Simeon's words when she presents Jesus in the Temple;[24] she does not understand, according to her own testimony, the answer given by Jesus when she finds him in the Temple among the teachers.[25] Elizabeth proclaims her blessed because of her faith.[26] Now, faith is consent not to something one sees, but above all to Someone who sees, to God who sees. Paul speaks of the "obedience of faith."[27] Such was Mary's faith. Mary was perfect in her obedience. And a humble servant.

## Jesus-Servant

The title of *doulos, doulē* in its threefold meaning of slave, servant, and child, which describes the most profound aspect of Mary's religion, likewise applies to Jesus' messianic vocation. The spiritual environment in which Scripture places this title is that of the prophecies concerning the Servant of Yahweh in the Book of Isaiah.[28]

### Jesus-Slave

In his Letter to the Philippians (2:6-11), Paul quotes an ancient hymn—to which he probably gave a personal touch—which relates what we can call the "story" of Jesus expressed in a human way. This hymn has been called *Christuslied.*[29] It evokes his divine condition (v. 6), his entry into the human condition, his condition of *slave* (v. 7), his extreme humiliation even to death on the cross (v. 8). In this hymn, Jesus is presented as a *slave*. Crucifixion itself,

22. 2 Cor 5:7.
23. Luke 1:29.
24. Luke 2:33.
25. Luke 2:50.
26. Luke 1:49.
27. Rom 1:5.
28. The four songs of the Servant (Isa 42:1-9; 49:1-6; 50:4-11; 52:13–53:12) speak of this Servant, whose personality is at once individual and collective. His personality is difficult to pinpoint. See Grelot, *Les poèmes.* On the presence of the Servant in the Synoptics, see Deiss, *Synopse,* 412.
29. J. Gnilka, *Der Philipperbrief,* Herders Kommentar (1968) 111.

among Greeks as well as among Romans, was in any case the punish-
ment reserved for slaves.[30]

### Jesus-Child

In two texts, Jesus is also called *pais* (child) without any explanation. This archaic title is found in the discourse Peter delivered after
healing the crippled beggar at the Beautiful Gate. Peter declares that
the God of the ancestors "glorified" his *"child,"* "sent" his *"child"*
in order to bless the people of the Covenant (Acts 3:13, 26).[31] (The
allusion is probably to the Servant of Yahweh, called *pais* in the
Septuagint.)

### Jesus, Servant and Son

Finally, we possess a group of texts which clearly affirm that
Jesus assumed the vocation of the Servant of Yahweh.[32] The most
significant testimony is that of Matthew 12:18-21, which quotes the
first song of the Servant in Isaiah 42:1-4:

> Here is my servant, whom I have chosen,
>     my beloved, with whom my soul is well
>         pleased,
> I will put my Spirit upon him. . . .
> And in his name the Gentiles will hope.

Jesus' messianic ministry fulfilled "what had been spoken through
the prophet Isaiah." Jesus was definitely the Servant chosen by God,
the beloved on whom the Spirit rested.

Now, it is this same text that is the basis for the story of Jesus'
baptism, especially for the voice from heaven. Indeed, the opening
words can be translated as either "my servant" or "my son" since
the term "servant" (*ebed* in Hebrew, *pais* in Greek) can mean "son."
This interpretation expresses fittingly the messianic vocation of Jesus,

---

30. *ThWNT*, 7:573.

31. The NRSV translates *pais* as "servant" here.

32. Readers will find the Synoptic references to the Servant in Deiss, *Synopse*, 412.
Other references: Isa 52:15 is quoted in Rom 15:21; Isa 53:1, in Rom 10:16; Isa 53:9,
in 1 Pet 2:22. On the title "Lamb of God" in John 1:29, 36, which probably evokes
the Servant according to Isa 53:7, see A. Jaubert, *Approches de l'Evangile de Jean*,
Parole de Dieu (Paris: Seuil, 1976) 135-39.

Servant of God—particularly throughout his messianic ministry—
and the One who was "declared to be Son of God with power according to the spirit of holiness by resurrection from the dead."[33]

After the resurrection, the early community projected its faith
in Christ, Son of God, into the baptism accounts. The "voice from
heaven" is different in each gospel, which confirms the very richness of the tradition. According to Mark 1:11, the voice is directly
addressed to Jesus, "You are my Son, the Beloved; with you I am
well pleased." In Matthew 3:17, it is addressed to the Christian community which contemplates its Messiah and says to it, "This is my
Son, the Beloved, with whom I am well pleased." Lastly, according to Luke 3:22, it reveals the divine filiation of Jesus by quoting
Psalm 2:7, "You are my son; today I have begotten you."[34]

We may understand the voice from heaven as an interior revelation.[35] Indeed, if this voice had been audible or if the opening of
the sky and the dove mentioned by the Gospels had been visible,
we would not understand how it is that later on John the Baptist
wondered about the true identity of Jesus and sent emissaries to
ask, "Are you the one who is to come, or are we to wait for another?"[36]

Can we imagine what really happened in Jesus' consciousness
at his baptism? We so often remain at the door of our own hearts
without understanding ourselves. Would we be capable of understanding Jesus' vocation?

This inner "vision" seems to correspond to the initial visions
that marked the vocations of the prophets, such as that of Moses
at the Burning Bush, Isaiah in the Temple with the song of the ser-
aphs, Ezekiel on the banks of the river Chebar seeing the heavens

33. Rom 1:4.

34. The version which quotes Ps 2:7 is a variant in the Western tradition. To these
references we may add Isa 63:19, which recalls the opening of the heavens in Mark
1:11, and Isa 63:11-14, which evokes the figure of Moses, the bearer of the Spirit. Concerning the texts quoted by the heavenly voice, F. Lentzen-Deis writes, "We must accept a 'living tradition' which freely combines different motifs, a storyteller who
introduces Old Testament themes without meaning to allude to any one definite Old
Testament text." F. Lentzen-Deis, *Die Taufe Jesu nach den Synoptikern* (Frankfurt am
Main: J. Knecht, 1970) 193.

35. Boismard, *Synopse*, 2:83. The tradition represented by the Targum believed
that at the sacrifice of Isaac by his father, a voice, coming from heaven had likewise
been heard and had said, "Come, see my two [persons] unique in my universe." See
Le Déaut, *Targum du Pentateuque*, 1:218.

36. Matt 11:3; Luke 7:19.

open before his eyes.[37] Nothing leads us to think that Jesus fore-
saw this vision or desired it. We can say that at his baptism, Jesus
received from heaven his investiture as Servant of Yahweh or else
that he deepened the awareness he already had of it. This vocation
of servant is in any case that of every believer since the Servant
represented the people of the Covenant.[38] Every believer is called
to fulfill this vocation. But Jesus was to fulfill it according to his
unique and transcendent charism.

The Letter to the Hebrews states that Jesus "learned obedience."[39]
In effect, the vocation of servant is a vocation of obedience. At the
beginning of his ministry, in the period called "the Galilean Spring,"
Jesus proclaimed the reign of the Beatitudes with enthusiasm, multiplied healings as if, like the Servant, he were taking upon himself
the sufferings and infirmities of his people.[40] Peter, who was an eye-
witness of the Galilean Spring, summed it up this way, "He went
about doing good."[41] Perhaps, in the intoxication of messianic joy,
Jesus was hoping to bring about the triumph of the coming reign
without obstacle. But as the opposition, then the hatred, of some
of the scribes, some of the Pharisees, and the priests arose against
him, he understood that he would also have to live the last of the
Songs of the Servant, the one that speaks of his suffering and death.
It is at this point that the transfiguration took place. Once more,
the heavenly voice declared that he was the beloved Son of the Father and thus renewed the messianic investiture.[42] It was also "from
that time on"[43] that Jesus began to foretell his passion. Then, Jesus
set forth, without any possible return, on the way to Calvary.

This obedience to the Father retained a fully human character.
It was dazzling in its authenticity. Sometimes it resembled a struggle,
as in the agony in the garden on the Mount of Olives. It always
ended with victory, the victory of submission through love. Thus,
after the first announcement of the passion, Peter intervened in order
to snatch Jesus from death, he thought, and save him against his

---

37. Exod 3:1-12; Isa 6:1-8; Ezek 1:1.
38. According to Isa 49:3. See also Isa 44:21.
39. Heb 5:8. K. Rahner writes, "In his human consciousness, Jesus did not know
everything. . . . [Such is] the faith conviction concerning Jesus' true humanity." K.
Rahner, *Aimer Jésus*, Jésus et Jésus-Christ 24 (Paris: Desclée de Brouwer, 1985) 112, 114.
40. Matt 8:17.
41. Acts 10:38.
42. Matt 17:5. See Mark 9:7; Luke 9:35.
43. Matt 16:21, after Peter's confession; Matt 17:1, six days later.

will, "God forbid it, Lord! This must never happen to you." Jesus repulsed him with very harsh words, "Get behind me, Satan! You are a stumbling block to me; for you are setting your mind not on divine things but on human things."[44] But, when the passion was upon him in the Garden of Olives, when it was at hand, Jesus begged his Father "with loud cries and tears"[45] to take away this cup of suffering, "Abba, Father, for you all things are possible; remove this cup from me."[46] All this shows that as long as suffering seems to lie in a faraway future, we accept it. But when it gets close to us and wants to grasp us in its claws, we push it back. Jesus was really like us in all things.

### Nazareth, the House of Obedience

Joseph is silent love and obedient love. Mary is the humble servant of the Lord. Jesus is the Servant whose obedience is the path of love toward the Father. Was the home in Nazareth the house where each one, imitating the others, learned obedience?

In fact, Jesus' word, "My food is to do the will of him who sent me," his affirmation, "I always do what is pleasing to him," his jubilation, "Yes, Father, for such was your gracious will,"[47] all these avowals, which were first heard in the Galilean countryside and then spread to the entire world to fill it throughout the ages with obedience and love toward the Father, are like the echo of the word which Mary pronounced in the house in Nazareth, "Let it be with me according to your word." Mary, the servant, was the ideal of obedient love for the child Jesus. And Jesus, the Servant, dying on the cross, led his mother after him into the supreme obedience, the total self-abandonment into the Father's hands. As in a choral composition by Bach, in which the melody is stated in turns by the soprano, alto, tenor, and bass voices and in which all these harmonically intertwined melodies are the background against which the musical piece unfolds in slow notes within a universe of splendor, so each of Jesus' thoughts, each of his words, each of his actions were variations on this single prayer, "Abba, Father . . . not

44. Matt 16:22-23.
45. Heb 5:7.
46. Mark 14:36.
47. John 4:34; 8:29. See also 5:30. Matt 11;29; Luke 10:21 (hymn of jubilation).

what I want, but what you want."[48] And this "what you want" was also the glorification on Easter morning. The song of obedience opened into the resurrection.

Father Lagrange wrote, "If we were allowed to push this far the analysis of [Jesus'] human development, we could say that there was in him, as in so many others, something of his mother's influence."[49] These are wise words. We must add that there was also something of his father's influence. . . . For Mary, as we have kept repeating, is not without Joseph and Joseph is not without Mary: such was God's will. And both are not without Jesus.

48. Mark 14:36.
49. M.-J. Lagrange, *L'Evangile de Jésus-Christ*, Etudes Bibliques (Paris: Gabalda, 1928) 50–51.

# Chapter 3

# At Nazareth, in Galilee

[Joseph] went away to the district of Galilee. There he made his home in a town called Nazareth. (Matt 2:22-23)

If we except the stay in Egypt to escape King Herod's fury—we do not know the duration of this stay—if we also except the times devoted to the pilgrimages to Jerusalem, the "hidden life" of Jesus, that is, his childhood, his adolescence, and his adulthood until thirty, took place entirely in the setting of the little village of Nazareth.[1]

At the time, Nazareth was an unimportant town. It was dwarfed by Sepphoris, a nearby city one-hour's walk to the north, an administrative and military center, which Herod Antipas had rebuilt. Furthermore, Nazareth could not boast of any biblical past, being mentioned neither in the Old Testament nor in the Talmud, nor in the Mishnah, nor in the writings of Flavius Josephus (ca. 37–ca.100). Outside the New Testament texts, the first mention of Nazareth is in an inscription in Caesarea, going back to the third or fourth century.[2]

The religious environment was principally marked by the influence of the Pharisees and Sadducees. Among the *Pharisees*, there were two schools: that of Hillel, liberal in character, and that of Shammai, whose interpretation of the Law was strict and rigid. There is no evidence that the religious peace of the Nazareth folks was disturbed by scholarly debates. Moreover, when Jesus was invited later on to state his position on the question of divorce, he avoided being drawn into the controversy between Hillel and Sham-

---

1. There are other spellings in the Synoptics: Nazaret and Nazara.
2. G. Vermes, "Jesus the Jew," *Jesus' Jewishness*, ed. J. H. Charlesworth (New York: The American Interfaith Institute-Crossroad, 1991) 110.

mai by appealing to the will of God "from the beginning of creation."[3] The *Sadducees* were a politico-religious group whose
members were recruited mostly from the priestly families and the
aristocracy. We know that they denied the resurrection of the dead
and the existence of angels.[4] They must have been of little importance in the village of Nazareth. As to the influence of the Essenes
of Qumran, we may surmise that it was no stronger in the religious
practice in Nazareth than in the whole of Judaism.[5]

All we know with certainty about the religious practice of the
Holy Family, is that it faithfully observed the Law of the Lord. When
recounting the episode of the presentation of Jesus in the Temple,
Luke points out this faithfulness to the Law three times.[6] On this
point, Joseph and Mary resembled Zechariah and Elizabeth, of
whom it is said that "both of them were righteous before God, living blamelessly according to all the commandments and regulations
of the Lord."[7]

Therefore, it was in Nazareth, an obscure village—and also in
God's deepest secret—far from the political and religious agitation
of the world, that the personality of the one who would be called
Rabbi Yeshua ben Yoseph from Nazareth, "Jesus son of Joseph from
Nazareth,"[8] was built, the one who, through the sole power of his
love, was going to set the world aflame by the fire of his gospel.
The development of his personality took place under the sun of
heavenly grace, of course, in his most intimate conversation with
his Father, but also in the warmth of the home of his father Joseph
and his mother Mary. His intelligence and his heart, like every
human being's, remained subjected to the human law of growth.

We possess no other sources than the Gospels for our knowledge of this growth. All we can do is seek to divine the marvels
of the hidden life from the marvels of the public life. In the fullness
of his adulthood, and at the peak of his Messianic vocation, Jesus
carried within himself, like all human beings, the indelible traces
of his childhood.

3. Mark 10:6; cf. Matt 19:4.
4. Cf. Matt 22:23; Mark 12:18; Luke 20:27; Acts 23:6. On the Pharisees, see note
7, pp. 52–53.
5. The influence of Philo of Alexandria (ca. 20 B.C.E.) was especially strong in
the Greek communities of the Diaspora.
6. Luke 2:22-24.
7. Luke 1:6.
8. John 1:45.

## CHILDHOOD MEMORIES

Jesus urged his disciples to become again like children. According to Jesus, this spiritual pilgrimage to the "golden age" of childhood—which stands in complete contrast to infantilism but stringently demands humility—is the very condition for entrance into the reign.

> Truly I tell you, unless you change and become like children, you will never enter the kingdom of heaven.[1]

At age thirty, in the full maturity of his intelligence and will, when he proclaimed the reign of heaven with a sovereign authority that astounded the crowds,[2] when he "muzzled"[3] both the unclean spirits which screamed and the storm which howled on the Sea of Galilee, Jesus kept a child's soul. His memory often brought him back to Nazareth, near Joseph and Mary. Certainly, he announced the good news through oracles, sayings, proverbs, blessings, and curses, according to the rich tradition of the prophets of old, but he used parables with predilection. Now, a number of his parables were stamped by his childhood memories, which then resurfaced in his heart.

### Mary's Bread

Bread was the staple food in Israel. To say "to take one's meal," one simply said "to eat bread." Mark relates that Jesus and his disciples were so beset by the crowd that "they could not even eat bread."[4]

Bread-making was an important task in Mary's daily life. She began by grinding the grain. She sat on her heels facing the grindstone. This was made of two superposed stones: the central cone of the lower stone fitted into the upper stone which had an opening into which the grain was poured. In order to turn the grindstone, it was better to have two people working together. Jesus evoked

---

1. Matt 18:3.
2. Matt 7:28-29; Mark 1:22; Luke 4:32.
3. *Phimoun* ("to muzzle") in Mark 1:25 and 4:39.
4. Mark 3:20, according to the Greek.

a familiar scene in Nazareth when he described the sudden coming of the Son of Man.

> There will be two women grinding meal together; one will be taken and the other left.[5]

The making of bread dough is always a delight for children. Mary prepared the dough in the evening for the bread of the next day. She placed it on a cloth in a basket made of braided reeds or in a wooden plate made by Joseph and covered it with another cloth. The next day, all the dough had risen. "How? During the night?" the child asked. Mary explained, "Long, long ago, when Sarah welcomed the three mysterious guests by the oaks of Mamre, she took three *seahs*[6] (measures) of flour, one for each guest. It was a lot. Enough for a festive banquet.[7] And yet the whole mass was raised. That's how strong the leaven is."

Jesus would remember Sarah and Mary, the Nazareth breadmaker. When he wanted to explain the irresistible power of the reign, he said,

> The kingdom of heaven is like yeast that a woman took and mixed in with three measures of flour until all of it was leavened.[8]

If the bread was prepared too far ahead of time, it risked becoming sour and moldy. Mary baked it every day, except on the Sabbath. When a visitor arrived unannounced in the evening and there was no bread left, people quickly ran to their neighbor's to borrow some: "Friend, lend me three loaves of bread; for a friend of mine has arrived, and I have nothing to set before him." Mary taught Jesus that we must ask God every day for that day, "Give us each day our daily bread."[9]

### The Mending Lesson

When a tunic or cloak was torn, Mary mended it. She would sit on her mat, take the garment in her hands, and examine it. The

5. Luke 17:35.
6. Gen 18:2, 6.
7. The *seah* was roughly equivalent to half a bushel (see Strack-Billerbeck, 1:669); therefore, three *seahs* were equivalent to about one and a half bushels.
8. Matt 13:33; Luke 13:20-21.
9. Luke 11:5 and 3.

child observed his mother. What was she about to do? In children's judgments, grownups sometimes have strange, unforeseeable ways of behaving. Why did she take this old and worn patch, which surely would not last very long, to mend this old cloak? Why did she not take this new and much prettier patch? Then, Mary explained,

> No one sews a piece of unshrunk cloth on an old cloak; otherwise the patch pulls away from it, the new from the old, and a worse tear is made.[10]

Jesus would not forget the mending lesson. Between rigid Pharisaism and gospel newness, there was not only difficulty of adaptation but total incompatibility. The good news could not be a patching up of the robe of a certain kind of Judaism, ill-clad in its inflexibly observed but unexamined ancient customs. The new wine of the gospel could not be poured into the old wineskins of human traditions, which were not intended for new circumstance. And Jesus concluded with a smile, "But one puts new wine into fresh wineskins."[11]

Mary took great care of the clothes. She would take them out of the closet at regular intervals and attentively examine them to be sure that the moths had not eaten them; then she would hang them up in the sun.

Later on, Jesus would teach,

> Store up for yourselves treasures in heaven, where neither moth nor rust consumes.[12]

### Joseph's Bushel

When Joseph's customers came to get some article they had ordered, they asked, "How much do I owe you?" Joseph answered, "One bushel of wheat." But there are bushels and bushels. There is the bushel scantily measured, and there is the bushel packed tightly, shaken together, running over.

Later on, Jesus remembered the bushels which Joseph earned and which were put into his lap, that is, his apron. He said,

10. Mark 2:21; Matt 9:16; Luke 5:36.
11. Mark 2:22; Matt 9:16-17; Luke 5:36-38.
12. Matt 6:20; Luke 12:33.

Give, and it will be given to you. A good measure, pressed down, shaken together, running over, will be put into your lap; for the measure you give will be the measure you get back.[13]

The passive "will be put into your lap" is the "divine passive." It was used to avoid, through reverence, pronouncing the divine name. The meaning is obviously, "Give and God will give to you."

There were similar traditional sayings which the child must have heard. "The measure with which a person measures, (God) will use to measure that person."[14] There remains however a fundamental difference between Jesus' saying and the traditional one.[15] Indeed, Jesus' words are directly prefaced by the law of mercy, "Be merciful, just as your Father is merciful," and by the universal prohibition against judging, "Do not judge, and you will not be judged."[16] The only judgment allowed by Jesus' new law is that of mercy.

## At the Market

The child Jesus loved to accompany Joseph and Mary when they went to market. It was the hub of the little town's life. The market *(agora)* or the public square *(plateia)* was like a fair: there were so many things to discover, to admire.

Mary had taught Jesus to greet everyone as a well-bred little boy is supposed to do. It is said of Rabbi Jochanan (d. ca. 80) that he was always the first to greet those he met on his way, even if they were pagans.[17] We may suppose that there were many pious and humble teachers like Rabbi Jochanan in Jesus' time. Later on, Jesus urged his disciples to welcome everyone with kindliness, "If you greet only your brothers and sisters, what more are you doing than others? Do not even the Gentiles do the same?"[18]

In the public squares, one met "the poor, the crippled, the blind, and the lame,"[19] the whole retinue of the unfortunate who were ask-

---

13. Luke 6:38; cf. Mark 4:24.
14. Strack-Billerbeck, 1:444.
15. A. Schlatter, *Der Evangelist Matthäus* (Stuttgart: Calwer Verlag, 1957) 241.
16. Luke 6:36-37.
17. Strack-Billerbeck, 1:382.
18. Matt 5:47.
19. Luke 14:21.

ing for alms. One could also see day laborers seeking employment. Those who were hired at the third hour (nine in the morning), therefore those who were to bear the burden of the day and the heat, would they receive a higher wage than those who just lent a hand toward evening? Joseph explained, "It all depends on the master. But when the Master is our God of tenderness and pity, each one receives what infinite kindness gives." In the parable of the laborers in the vineyard, Jesus remembered the Nazareth day laborers: they were all paid according to the master's kindness.[20]

News of the village was exchanged. Some people took advantage of the idle bystanders, a captive audience, to preach in the public square,[21] as still happens today with soapbox orators. There were also certain scribes and Pharisees who strutted about in fine apparel[22] and savored the pleasure of being greeted with the title of "Rabbi."[23] How broad their phylacteries were and how long their tassels[24] compared to those Joseph wore! Moreover, Joseph dressed thus only for prayer. Occasionally, certain of their number would install themselves in the middle of the public square in order to be seen at their devotions.[25] Joseph had taught the child, "Those who pray do not offer themselves as a public show. When they address their heavenly Father, they 'go into [their] room and shut the door' and praise the Father in secret.[26] True servants—those of whom the scroll of Isaiah speaks—hold themselves in humility and reserve; they do not lift their 'voice in the streets.' "[27]

At the market, there were sparrows for sale. The prices varied: two sparrows for a penny, according to Matthew, or five for two

---

20. Matt 20:1-16.
21. Cf. Luke 10:9-10.
22. Mark 12:38; Luke 20:46.
23. Matt 23:6; Luke 11:43.
24. Matt 23:5. The phylacteries (from the Greek *phulaktērion*, "protection") were small capsules containing excerpts from the Law. They were worn on the forehead and the left wrist, according to a literal interpretation of Exod 13:9. The tassels or fringes were also prescribed in the Law (Num 15:37-41; Deut 22:12) to remind the wearers to keep the commandments. They were worn on the four corners of the prayer garment (shawl) or cloak. In the beginning, they probably were amulets (like those represented on ancient Egyptian monuments) to which a religious meaning in relation with the Law was later added.
25. Matt 6:5.
26. Matt 6:6, quoting Isa 26:20.
27. Matt 12:19, quoting Isa 42:2.

pennies, according to Luke,[28] which was a better buy. The poor birds had been captured in the fowler's net or by the hunter's slingshot. Mary explained to the child, "Our God—who is forever blessed[29]—gave them for food to humankind. However, God's Providence watches over them. Not one of them is forgotten by God."

Jesus remembered the sparrows sold at the market, two for one penny or five for two pennies. He taught,

> Not one of them is forgotten in God's sight. . . . Do not be afraid; you are of more value than many sparrows.[30]

## With the Boys and Girls of Nazareth

Jesus seems to have fitted in well with the Nazareth children. He knew their games. He also knew that in each group there are some members who are of a contrary disposition. When the group wants to play wedding and dance, they want to weep as at a funeral. When the group wants to play funeral and wail, they want to dance. And, of course, a quarrel ensues.

> We played the flute for you, and
> you did not dance;
> we wailed, and you did not mourn.[31]

Jesus remembered the children's games on the public square. He reproached the people of his generation on account of their inconsistency and levity: the reign is here, at the door; like a net, judgment is about to fall on them; and they are quibbling! "John came in penance, neither eating nor drinking, and you did not listen to him. The Son of Man came in joy and you rejected him. You are behaving like insufferable children. Whoever the messengers God sends you, you have no regard for them. Whatever their messages, you criticize them."[32]

---

28. Matt 10:29; Luke 12:6. "Penny" translates the Greek word *assarion*, which was a Roman copper coin worth, in Jesus' time, the sixteenth of a denarius. The denarius was the daily wage of a field laborer (Matt 20:2).

29. The custom was to add this blessing to God's name; see Rom 9:5.

30. Luke 12:6.

31. Matt 11:16; Luke 7:31-32. See Jeremias, *Paraboles*, 160–62.

32. Cf. Matt 11:18-19; Luke 7:33-34.

There is an amusing difference between Luke's text and Matthew's. Less well informed of Galilean customs than Matthew, or else not too interested in them, Luke has the boys calling to one another, as if all participants played the same role. But the role of mourner was for women, whereas round dances and other dances at weddings were chiefly the province of men. Matthew makes a distinction: certain boys reserved for themselves "the least tiring roles, flute-playing or wailing, leaving to their playmates the more strenuous ones."[33]

### The Houses in Nazareth

Nazareth houses have a lot to teach us. They are the natural setting for many a gospel scene.

Some of the houses were like caves. Barely a century ago, it was possible to write, "A certain number of houses are built against the mountain, against the limestone rock; and in this rock, which is quite soft, there sometimes are, at the back of the houses, caves, either natural or artificially enlarged. Some people even dwell in simple caves."[34] In the community of the Sisters of Nazareth, it is still possible today to visit a group of buildings backed against the mountain where "the dwelling of the Just One"[35] was erected. The paved street which excavations have unearthed seems to go back to the first century. It is in that street that the child Jesus went to the fountain with Mary or played hopscotch with the other children of Nazareth.

Most of the modest houses were made of sun-dried bricks or straw. It was not difficult to break in through such walls. Later on, Jesus advised his listeners to store their treasures in heaven, "where thieves do not break in and steal." Luke perceived the difficulty his Greek readers would have had in imagining that one could break in through a stone wall. Therefore, he changed and simplified the phrase thus: "where no thief comes near."[36]

33. Jeremias, *Paraboles*, 161.
34. A. Legendre, "Nazareth," in *Dictionnaire de la Bible*, vol. 4, pt. 1 (Paris: Letouzey et Ané, 1928) col. 1527.
35. See J.-B. Livio, "Les fouilles chez les religieuses de Nazareth," *Le Monde de la Bible* 16 (1988) 28–36.
36. Cf. Matt 6:19 and Luke 12:33.

People were careful to build on a solid foundation, such as a rock or a stone wall. To build on sand was to ask for trouble. Indeed, in Palestine, the fall rains begin as early as October and reach their climax in January. If they were gentle, people said in Jesus' day that "God's rivers were preparing the ears of grain."[37] But now and then, there are extremely violent, stormy downpours in October.

Later on, Jesus spoke of rains which, having turned torrential, beat against a house built on sand. He added with emphasis, "and it fell—and great was its fall." Such would be the fate of foolish persons who heard his words without acting on them.[38]

In view of summer heat and winter cold—the average temperature in Nazareth is 72 in August, and 44 in January[39]—there were few windows and they were small. Large windows were regarded as signs of arrogance. Long ago, Jeremiah had condemned the ostentation of dwellings that boasted "large upper rooms" with "windows [cut out]."[40] The Galilean houses were dark. The floors were beaten earth. Jesus remembered a housewife who had lost a silver coin: she had lighted a lamp and carefully swept the house until she found it.[41]

A single door gave access to the house. Even a child knew that it was enough to have just one man, strong and well armed, to keep the whole household safe.[42]

A key was used to move the latch and open or close the lock. Whoever had the key had the power. "He shall open, and no one shall shut; he shall shut, and no one shall open," Isaiah had said concerning Eliakim, who had received the key of the house of David.[43] Later on, Jesus reproached the lawyers for having "taken away the key of knowledge." They had not entered the reign and they hindered others who were entering.[44]

37. Ps 65:10.

38. Matt 7:26-27; Luke 6:49. In 1861, in Nazareth, the winter rains caused the collapse of twenty-five Arab houses and a part of the house of hospitality for pilgrims. See P. Gaechter, *Das Matthäus Evangelium* (Innsbruck: Tyrolia, 1964) 251, n. 31.

39. See F.-M. Abel, *Géographie de la Palestine*, vol. 1, Etudes Bibliques (Paris: Gabalda, 1967) 110. Nazareth is classified in the mountainous zone; see p. 109, n. 2.

40. Jer 22:14.

41. Luke 15:8-10.

42. Luke 11:21; see Matt 12:29; Mark 3:27.

43. Isa 22:22.

44. Luke 11:52.

Canaanites liked to inscribe magical signs on the door jambs or hang amulets from them; they thought that these would repel malevolent spirits. Rather than try to extirpate this pagan custom, Deuteronomy 6:9 preferred to exorcise it by urging believers to "write . . . on the doorposts of your house and on your gates" excerpts from the Law. As a consequence, Joseph had fixed on the doorpost of his house a little cylinder containing a sacred text. When he went out or came back with the child, we can imagine him holding the little one in his arms and lifting him so that he could touch the sacred text with his hands. And he might have whispered with the child the prayer from the Psalm:

> The Lord will keep
>> your going out and your coming in
>> from this time on and forevermore.[45]

The roofs were generally flat. To build them, people put joists every twenty-seven to thirty-three inches. On top of these, they placed tangled branches and reeds mixed with mud. They rolled the roof to pack it down. Thanks to winter rains, grass grew and its roots bound the earth. This grass withered in the first heat of summer. Thus the wicked, according to Psalm 129:6, dry up as does the grass on the housetops when the desiccating desert wind blows. One went onto the roof by an outside staircase. Roofs were ideal places to exchange news from one house to the next. To proclaim on the housetop was to speak openly in front of the whole village. Jesus reminded his disciples in his missionary discourse:

> Therefore whatever you have said in the dark will be heard in the light, and what you have whispered behind closed doors will be proclaimed from the housetops.[46]

In his capacity as carpenter, Jesus certainly helped in the construction of these roofs. In any case, he was not surprised when, later on in Capernaum, people made a hole in the roof of the house where "he was speaking the word"[47] and lowered the paralytic on his mat in order to set him right at Jesus' feet. This is one of the

---

45. Ps 121:8.
46. Luke 12:3. The saying is a little different in Matt 10:27.
47. Mark 2:2-4. For his Greek readers, unfamiliar with Galilean roofs, Luke writes in 5:19 that the paralytic was let down "through the tiles."

most stunning scenes in the Gospels. We can picture Christ proclaiming the reign with sovereign authority, but surrounded by a cloud of dust—for one does not dismantle such a roof without a cloud of dust—sitting in the midst of the clumps of earth and branches fallen from the roof, and granting the paralytic the forgiveness of the Most High together with bodily healing. This is a sublime symbol of the mystery of the incarnation: heavenly grace meeting the dust of our earth.

### Where Do Babies Come From?

Like all children, Jesus must have asked one day, with the naíve spontaneity proper to children's questions, "Imma, where do babies come from?" Mary must have explained with simplicity, "Children are carried in their mothers' hearts. There they grow, and when the time comes, they are born." "Does the mother suffer for her child?" "Sometimes. God told Eve, 'I will greatly increase your pangs in childbearing; / in pain you shall bring forth children.' And according to the prophet, God declares in person that God suffers like a woman in labor, but it is to give birth to a new world from which all suffering will be banished.[48] The new world is born in suffering but opens onto joy. The new creature is born in suffering but opens onto life."

Later on, Jesus depicted the conditions of the messianic community in terms of childbirth. It would endure the sadness of its Messiah's passion. It would be radiant with joy when the new people were born in the Messiah's resurrection. The image of the woman in labor came back to his mind.

> When a woman is in labor, she has pain, because her hour has come. But when her child is born, she no longer remembers the anguish because of the joy of having brought a human being into the world. So you have pain now; but I will see you again, and your hearts will rejoice, and no one will take your joy from you.[49]

Childhood years are an inexhaustible source of memories. When Jesus preached the gospel, the simplest images of his childhood became revelations of the mystery of the reign of heaven.

---

48. Gen 3:16; Isa 42:14.
49. John 16:21-22. The text of Isa 66:5-14 must be the background for John's text, according to M.-E. Boismard and A. Lamouille, *Synopse des quatre Evangiles*, vol. 3 (Paris: Cerf, 1977) 388.

## AT THE HEART OF CREATION

You save humans and animals alike,
   O Lord.
How precious is your steadfast love,
   O God! (Ps 36:6-7)

Every child of Israel knew that after having purified the world in the waters of the flood, God had sealed God's covenant, not only with Noah and his descendants, but also with the whole of creation and especially with the animals. God had, so to speak, made a pact of friendship "with every living creature . . . the birds, the domestic animals, and every animal of the earth."[1]

Jesus lived in the very heart of this covenant. Creation was for him the epiphany of God's presence to humankind. The sky was "the throne of God"; the earth was God's "footstool." Jerusalem was for him "the city of the great King."[2] The lightning that "comes from the east and flashes as far as the west" evoked the dazzling suddenness of the day of the Son of Man.[3] The evening breeze that lazily tarried in the alleys of Jerusalem and bathed them in coolness was the sign of the Spirit which "blows where it chooses" and of which people "do not know where it comes from or where it goes."[4] Creation was like an immense palace in which every creature cried "Glory!"[5] Before the face of the Lord who is coming, it is said in the Psalms,[6] the sea roars with everything that fills it, the rivers clap their hands, the mountains shout for joy, the countryside exults with all its fruit, the forest trees dance with glee. . . . Jesus moved freely in this universe of signs where every creature sings to God and acclaims God's presence.

### Animals of the Galilean Countryside

The righteous know the needs
   of their animals. (Prov 12:10)

1. Gen 9:10.
2. Matt 5:34-35.
3. Matt 24:27; Luke 17:24.
4. John 3:8.
5. Ps 29:8.
6. Pss 96:11-12; 98:7-8.

Israel lived in a sort of familiarity with domestic animals. People liked to name their daughters after favorite animals, a custom which was flattering to their daughters: Rachel means "ewe"; Deborah, "bee." One of Job's daughters was called Dove (Jemimah).[7] The story of Tabitha, the devoted seamstress, is appealing. Tabitha is her Aramaic name. Luke translates, "which in Greek is Dorcas," (that is, "gazelle"); he wanted his readers to share his admiration for Dorcas, the gazelle, rich in "good works and acts of charity."[8]

This familiarity was lived in a climate of kindness, even cordiality. Thus, domestic animals, and particularly oxen and donkeys, had a right to the Sabbath rest, like every son and daughter of Israel.[9] It was forbidden to muzzle an ox while it was treading out the grain, that is, the animal had to be left free to eat to its heart's content while working.[10] When one discovered a bird's nest, one was forbidden to take both the mother and the young: "Let the mother go, taking only the young for yourself, in order that it may go well with you and you may live long."[11]

The most tender texts towards animals come from the Targum on Leviticus. Leviticus has several laws concerning animals that may be offered in sacrifice: it commands that the calf, the lamb, and the kid must not be separated from their mothers during the first eight days following birth; that the cow or the ewe must not be immolated with their young on the same day. And the sublime reason given—it was added in the Aramaic text to the translation of the original Hebrew—is the following:

> My people, children of Israel,
>   you must be merciful on earth
>   as I am merciful in heaven.[12]

Therefore, God's mercy surrounded all God's creatures, humans and animals. And it was by practicing this mercy towards animals that the faithful imitated the heavenly Father's mercy. In the gospel, this mercy of God towards animals becomes the supreme rule of

7. Job 42:14.
8. Acts 9:36.
9. Exod 13:12; Deut 5:14.
10. Deut 25:4.
11. Deut 22:6-7.
12. Targum of Leviticus 22:27-28. See Le Déaut, *Targum*, 2:475.

Christian conduct towards brothers and sisters: "Be merciful, just as your Father is merciful."[13]

## The Hen and Her Chicks and the Rooster

The child Jesus grew up in the environment of a village of the Galilean countryside. With him the familiar village animals seem to enter the gospel and play their part in the service of the announcement of the reign.

How often he saw the hen gathering her brood under her wings to protect them from danger! How often he desired to gather his people, as the hen gathers her chicks, to protect them from the impending catastrophe![14]

People thought that God had bestowed a special intelligence on the rooster.[15] Indeed, every morning, he knew how to awaken dawn and announce the sun. It was the rooster which later on woke up Peter, about to sink into the slumber of his denial, and drew from his heart a spring of bitter tears.[16]

## "Innocent as Doves"

Often families owned a little dovecote, as is still the custom in the villages of Syria and Egypt, to raise doves and turtledoves. The animals could become the offering of the poor in the Temple.[17] They could also enhance a festive meal.

Israel had a good opinion of doves. The bridegroom of the Song of Songs never tires of saying that his "dove" is absolutely without compare, that her eyes are enchanting as "doves beside springs of waters."[18] Jesus remembered the doves which lived familiarly among the people of Nazareth. When he sent his disciples "like sheep in the midst of wolves" at the time of the Galilean mission, he cautioned them to be "innocent as doves."[19]

13. Luke 6:36. On the whole of the Palestinian fauna, see Abel, *Géographie*, 219, 233. On the animals mentioned in the Bible, see S. Many's article in *Dictionnaire de la Bible*, vol. 1, pt. 1 (Paris: Letouzey et Ané, 1926) cols. 603–24.

14. Matt 23:37; Luke 13:34.

15. According to Job 38:36 (JB).

16. Matt 26:75; Mark 14:72; Luke 22:62.

17. Luke 22:4; Matt 21:12; Mark 11:15; John 2:14, 16.

18. Cant 5:12; 6:9.

19. Matt 10:16. "Simple" (*akeraios*, literally "unmixed").

### The Puppies

Jesus was familiar with young dogs which watched for crumbs that fell under the table. During festive meals, people wiped their fingers with the soft part of the bread or with flat bread. The whole thing was then thrown under the table. The puppies were on the lookout for these morsels.

We remember that puppies are mentioned in the story of the Canaanite woman.[20] What an admirable mother! To persuade Jesus to cure her daughter who "had an unclean spirit" (Mark), she was ready to accept all sorts of humiliation. She, *kunarion* ("puppy"), dares to implore the *Kurios*, the Lord. Exasperated by her cries, the apostles stepped in, "Send her away [literally, "untie her"], for she keeps shouting after us." Jesus refused to answer her plea. He had been sent only to the lost sheep of the house of Israel, not to pagan girls, even to deliver them from unclean spirits. It was a question of principle: "It is not fair to take *[labein]* the children's food and throw *[balein]* it to the dogs." She continued her supplications. What would a mother not do for her daughter? And finally, Jesus granted her, not a few crumbs that fell from the table, but the children's bread. He admired her faith and cured her daughter.[21]

### The Young Ravens

Children all over the world are attracted to birds' nests, particularly in the spring when the nests are atwitter with the young birds' chirping. What a marvel is the stork's nest, woven in the tops of fir trees,[22] or the songbird's, hung in giant trees, or the eagle's, "set among the stars."[23] But who fed the young birds?

Mary probably explained to the child that according to Scripture, it is God who "provides for the raven its prey/ when its young ones cry to God."[24] This is what is sung in the Psalm:

---

20. Matt 15:21-28 and Mark 7:24-30. On the puns in the Greek text, see J.-P. Charlier, *Jésus au milieu de son peuple*, Lire la Bible 78 (Paris: Cerf, 1987) 148-49.

21. Dogs are also mentioned in the saying of Matt 7:6, "Do not give what is holy to dogs," and in the parable of the rich man and Lazarus in Luke 16:21. The dogs in question are street dogs for which Jesus showed the repulsion Israelites had toward them.

22. Ps 104:17.

23. Obad 4.

24. Job 38:41.

> Sing to the Lord with thanksgiving;
>> make melody to our God on the lyre. . . .
> He gives to the animals their food,
>> and to the young ravens when they cry.[25]

In return, ravens rendered services to humans. Ravens brought food to the prophet Elijah when, fleeing for his life from King Ahab, he went into hiding near the Wadi Cherith, not far from Nazareth. "The ravens brought him bread and meat in the morning, and bread and meat in the evening."[26]

The Lord remembered the young ravens of Nazareth. He had them triumphantly enter the first sermon in Luke under the heading "Providence."

> Consider the ravens: they neither sow nor reap . . . and yet God feeds them. Of how much more value are you than the birds![27]

In recording this saying, Matthew omitted the mention of ravens. Perhaps he feared they might detract from the solemnity of the Messiah. Therefore he changed them to commonplace "birds of the air." As a good Israelite, he might also have remembered that the Law classifies ravens among unclean animals.[28] But Luke preserved the most faithful echo of Jesus' words.

### Foxes and Vultures

On the Sabbath, Joseph, Mary, and the child could take a walk whose length did not exceed what is called "a sabbath day's journey."[29] Interpreting a text from Exodus 16:29, tradition has determined this journey to be two thousand cubits, that is, about two thirds of a mile. But, at the same time, it indicates juridical exceptions which allow a longer distance without infraction of the Sabbath rest.

25. Ps 147:7, 9.

26. 1 Kgs 17:4, 6. The Wadi Cherith is sometimes identified with the Wadi el-Yabis, a tributary of the Jordan on its left bank which joins the Jordan about nineteen miles from Nazareth as the crow flies.

27. Luke 12:24.

28. Matt 6:26; Lev 11:15.

29. Acts 1:12 states that the distance separating Mount Olivet from Jerusalem is "a sabbath day's journey." The Mishnah treats of the sabbath day's journey in the treatise Erubin 4:3, 7.

Joseph might have shown the child the den of a fox in a thicket or, anchored to the rocks, the nest of a vulture.

Can one imagine a bird without a nest? Can one imagine a person without a home? However, such would be Jesus' situation. He remembered the foxes' dens and the birds' nests in the Nazareth countryside.

> Foxes have holes, and birds of the air have nests; but the Son of Man has nowhere to lay his head.[30]

Vultures evoked landscapes of ruins and desolation, even of carnage.[31] Impossible to hide the carcass of an animal in the countryside: the circling of vultures in the sky betrayed it. In the same way, impossible to hide the coming of the Son of Man:

> For as the lightning comes from the east and flashes as far as the west, so will be the coming of the Son of Man. Wherever the corpse is, there the vultures will gather.[32]

### Snakes and Scorpions

Snakes are particularly numerous in Palestine. Thirty-three species are known to live there.[33] Some are highly venomous, like the cobra or the horned viper. Joseph had forewarned the child, "When the peace of the first Paradise returns, the nursling will be able to play where the asp lives and the weaned child will be able to put its hand on the adder's den;[34] but today, as long as humankind is not at peace with the rose, that is, as long as roses have thorns, one must beware of snakes and their deadly poison.

The doings of certain scribes and Pharisees, when they opposed the newness of the gospel, were also a deadly poison. They were in truth the "descendants of those who murdered the prophets." Jesus upbraided them,

> You snakes, you brood of vipers! How can you escape being sentenced to hell?[35]

30. Luke 9:58; Matt 8:20.
31. Isa 34:15.
32. Matt 24:27-28; see Luke 17:24, 37.
33. M. Du Buit, "Palestine," in *Dictionnaire de la Bible, Supplément*, vol. 6 (Paris: Letouzey et Ané, 1960) col. 1049.
34. Isa 11:8.
35. Matt 23:31, 33; see Matt 12:34.

Jesus also knew scorpions. They can be as dangerous as the snakes. What father, if his "child asks for a fish, will give a snake instead of a fish? Or if the child asks for an egg, will give a scorpion?" And Jesus concluded,

> If you then, who are evil, know how to give good gifts to your children, how much more will the heavenly Father give the Holy Spirit to those who ask him![36]

The snake would again be mentioned when Jesus cautioned his disciples, at the time of the Galilean mission, to be "wise as serpents and innocent as doves."[37] The image is vivid and startling; the understanding of the saying, not easy. Luke must have shared this opinion for he evades the difficulty by omitting the saying. The horizon of the Galilean mission was a somber one. Opposition, hatred, and persecution threatened the missionaries. Therefore, let them be as wise[38] as snakes are supposed to be.

### The Sheep of Nazareth

The sheep *(probaton)* is the animal most often named in the Gospels: it is mentioned thirty-six times in thirty-two verses. This reveals its importance in the Galilean countryside.[39] It was precious for its milk, its skin, and especially its wool.

With every dawn, the narrow streets of Nazareth belonged to the sheep and goats. When a shepherd arrived at the sheepfold in the early morning, the sheep recognized the shepherd's voice. They raised their heads and thronged the door, ready to bound out in order to reach pasture. The child Jesus was familiar with the scene. The shepherd called each sheep *kat onoma* ("by name"). The shepherd led them all out, walking before them. The sheep followed

36. Luke 11:11-13; Matt 7:9-11.

37. Matt 10:16.

38. Matthew writes *phronimoi*, that is, "having heart," inasmuch as the heart is the seat of intelligence.

39. The Gospels have three words for "lamb": *amnos*, in John 1:29, 36; *arēn*, in Luke 10:3; *arnion*, in John 21:15. To designate the goats, Matthew uses the word *eriphion* in 25:33 and *eriphos* in 25:32. *Eriphos* occurs also in Luke 15:29, where it must be translated "kid." The wealth of the vocabulary indicates the importance of the theme.

the shepherd whose voice they knew. They would not have followed a stranger "because they do not know the voice of strangers."[40]

In a little village, where every wall had an ear and every door a tongue, the shepherds readily recounted among themselves the news of the day. Such and such a sheep had strayed: the shepherd had immediately gone in search of it and found it. Another had fallen into a crevice: it had been promptly lifted out even though it was the Sabbath.[41]

A shepherdless sheep is the very image of distress and loss. It cannot survive alone separated from the flock. Such would have been the case of the believer who abandoned the community. That one would perish, a "lost sheep of the house of Israel."[42]

In Nazareth, people had kept the memory of a shepherd—in fact, a hired hand—who had fled when he had seen the wolf coming. The true shepherd defended the sheep. The hired hand did not care for the sheep. And without a shepherd, the flock is scattered.[43]

In the evening, when the flock returned to the village, the shepherd separated the goats from the sheep. Indeed, goats do not tolerate the night chill and must therefore be housed in a covered shelter. Sheep, on the contrary, are able to spend the night in the open air. This sorting, the child thought, resembled a judgment.[44]

The Nazareth sheep have become almost familiar to us. They inspired many a comparison, and particularly, among those which are in the very heart of the gospel, the allegory of the Good Shepherd and the parable of the lost and found sheep. They will be part of the proclamation of the good news until the parousia.

### The Camel

As a child, Jesus had the opportunity to admire as they passed through the Galilean countryside, caravans of camels, which people imagined were similar to those of the Ishmaelites who, in the time of the patriarchs, had taken Joseph to Egypt as a slave.[45] In the wide horizon of the Galilean landscape, camels, ships of the desert, cut

40. John 10:3-5.
41. Matt 12:11; 18:12.
42. Matt 10:6; 15:24.
43. John 10:12-13; Matt 26:31; Mark 14:27.
44. Matt 25:32. See Jeremias, *Paraboles*, 196.
45. Gen 37:25.

a proud figure. But, in the narrow streets of Nazareth, especially if they were loaded with baskets and pouches filled with merchandise, they were a big nuisance.

Jesus observed them with a smile of amusement. He had a most vivid imagination; he mentioned camels twice in unforgettable phrases. The first one asserts that "it is easier for a camel to go through the eye of a needle than for someone who is rich to enter the kingdom of heaven."[46] The second one was directed at the "scribes and Pharisees, hypocrites." They insisted on insignificant details of the Law, but omitted the most serious points. Jesus told them that they strained out a gnat, but swallowed a camel (with its great hump!).[47]

### Joseph's She-donkey

Nowhere in the Gospels is there any word about Joseph's she-donkey.[48] However, it was there throughout his days, his labors, his comings and goings.

In Palestine, the jenny was the preferred mount. Its sure-footed negotiating of the rocky paths in the Palestinian hills and its endurance made it the indispensable companion of the Holy Family in all its travels. How else could Mary, then at the end of her pregnancy, have managed to journey from Nazareth to Bethlehem? As the crow flies, the distance is some sixty-two miles and travellers must almost double that figure when they use the trails connecting the villages. And how can we imagine the flight into Egypt without the help of a donkey when close to two hundred miles separate Bethlehem from the Egyptian frontier?

Does God love she-donkeys? Did Joseph's she-donkey play a part in the child's religious formation?

The Code of the Covenant, according to Exodus 23:5, has this sublime law,

> When you see the donkey of one who hates you lying under its burden and you would hold back from setting it free, you must help to set it free.

46. Matt 19:24; see Mark 10:25; Luke 18:25.
47. Matt 23:24; see Lev 11:4.
48. We speak of a she-donkey or jenny rather than simply a donkey. People preferred female donkeys to males because, on the one hand, they gave excellent milk

The sublimity of the law is this: God's love rests on all God's creatures; God cares for the donkey which falls under its load. Whoever claims to be faithful to the Covenant must come to the aid of the fallen animal, even if it is an enemy's: such is God's law.

If God thus loved donkeys, how could Jesus not have wanted to imitate the heavenly Father and love in particular the animal which was, in a real sense, part of his family?

The duty of bringing help to animals is so important in God's eyes that it takes precedence over the law of the Sabbath rest. Even on the Sabbath, Jesus said, one unties the donkey and the ox to take them to water. Even on the Sabbath, if an ox has fallen into the well, one must without delay pull it out.[49]

The last time a donkey is mentioned in Jesus' life is just before the accounts of the passion. At his messianic entrance into Jerusalem on Palm Sunday, Jesus chose for his mount, not the ceremonial horse, which would have been an unmistakable sign of his dignity, but simply a she-donkey. He thus fulfilled the prophecy made to the daughter of Zion:

> Look, your king is coming to you,
>   humble *[praus]* and mounted on a donkey,
>   and on a colt, the foal of a donkey.[50]

In biblical vocabulary, the adjective *praus* ("humble") is a synonym of *tapeinos* ("meek").[51] The she-donkey of Psalm Sunday reveals to the community the meekness and humility of its Messiah.

## Plants of the Galilean Countryside

Jesus' eyes reflected the Galilean countryside. And the Galilean countryside, in Jesus' eyes, reflected heaven. It is as if every created beauty spoke to him of the Father.

---

and, on the other, they were more tractable and less stubborn. In the enumeration of Job's riches, only she-donkeys are mentioned (1:3; 42:12).

49. Luke 13:15; 14:5.

50. Matt 21:5, quoting Isa 62:11 and Zech 9:9; see John 12:15. Let us note that the prophecy speaks of a donkey, not a she-donkey, but that Matthew, quoting the prophecy, speaks of a she-donkey.

51. C. Spicq, *Notes de Lexicographie, Supplément* (Göttingen: Vandenhoeck & Ruprecht, 1982) 577.

The seed which is sown in "good soil," that is, "in an honest and good heart," teaches us that the word of God can bear fruit up to a hundredfold.[52] The wheat which sprouts and ripens by itself under God's eyes while humans do nothing but "sleep and rise night and day" reveals the irresistible power of the gospel.[53] The lilies of the field, in their symphony of colors, sing the Father's Providence. The grass which blooms today and tomorrow is burned in the oven, but that which God clothes with splendor, preaches trust to people of weak faith. The reed which bends with the wind is an image of the precariousness and fragility of the powerful of this world.[54] The thunderbolt falling from heaven evokes the suddenness of Satan's fall.[55]

Who in the world had sown weeds into the wheat field? Was it not absolutely necessary to pull them out immediately? No. People must tolerate their presence in the middle of the wheat. They must also tolerate the fact that good and evil are mixed in the ecclesial community. But come harvest time at the end of the age . . . then the angels will sort out good from evil as one separates wheat from weeds.[56]

In a corner of the garden, Mary planted mint, dill, and cummin for kitchen use. The child asked his mother if it was necessary to tithe these plants. Mary had answered that one must be concerned with "justice and mercy and faith," without omitting the tithing.[57]

The mustard seed is "the smallest [or almost!] of all the seeds." But it could grow to the point of becoming "a tree" more than twelve feet tall. The extraordinary growth of the minute mustard seed was the very picture of the extraordinary growth of the reign. At least, such was Jesus' hope. Such also was to be his disciples' faith. Jesus told them:

52. Luke 8:8, 15. On the flora, see Abel, *Géographie*, 204–17. The *Letter of Aristeas* (ca. 200 B.C.E.), Sources Chrétiennes 89 (Paris: Cerf, 1962) 57, describes the Galilean countryside in these words: "It is entirely planted with numerous olive trees, cereals, vegetables, and also vineyards, and it abounds with honey. As for the fruit-bearing trees and the palm trees, it is impossible to count them in that region (pp. 159, 161). We must allow for some hyperbole in this description of the Galilean landscape. But it reflects what could be said about the lower Galilee where Nazareth is situated.

53. Mark 4:26-29.

54. Matt 6:29-30; Luke 12:27-28. Matt 11:7; Luke 7:24.

55. Luke 10:18.

56. Matt 13:24-30.

57. Matt 23:23.

If you have faith the size of a mustard seed, you will say to this mountain, "Move from here to there." and it will move; and nothing will be impossible for you.[58]

The fig tree is often mentioned in the New Testament (seventeen times; and twenty-six in the Old Testament). It was commonly planted close to grapevines, for its branches served as a trellis. The ideal of peace in Israel was for people to quietly sit "under their own vines and under their own fig trees."[59] For his comparisons and parables, Jesus often made use of the fig tree. Thus he said that one cannot hope to gather figs from thorns any more than one can find good fruit in false prophets.[60] And again, as surely as the fig tree's leaves announce the coming season, so would the ruin of the Temple announce the judgment of Israel.[61]

The Gospels also record the story of the cursed fig tree.[62] In the early morning, Jesus was going from Bethany to Jerusalem. It was the time of Passover, therefore spring (Mark explicitly notes that it was not the season for figs). Jesus was hungry. He approached the fig tree, found only leaves, cursed the tree, which withered. His disappointment at not finding figs symbolizes his disappointment at the sterility of the people who neglected to bear the fruits of conversion. His curse did not apply to Israel, but was intended as a supreme warning to awaken the people from their spiritual sleep.

Luke did not have the heart to report this story filled with such great sadness. Instead, he has the parable of "the last chance for the fig tree." For three years, the fig tree had not produced any fruit. The master ordered it cut down. The gardener suggested a delay out of clemency: "Sir, let it alone for one more year, until I dig around it and put manure on it. If it bears fruit next year, well and good; but if not, you can cut it down."[63] According to Leviticus,[64] when one plants a fruit tree, one refrains from picking its fruit for the first three years. The fig tree of the parable had remained barren

58. Matt 13:31-32; Mark 4:30-32; Luke 13:18-19. Matt 17:20; Luke 17:6.
59. Mic 4:4; Zech 3:10.
60. Luke 6:44.
61. Matt 24:32-34; Mark 13:28-30; Luke 21:29-32.
62. Matt 21:18-22 and Mark 11:12-14, 20. It is generally agreed that the two following sayings on faith and the efficacy of prayer (Matt 21:21-22; Mark 11:24) belong to another redactional level.
63. Luke 13:6-9.
64. Lev 19:23.

during the next three years. The last delay of grace granted to it was therefore the seventh year, the sabbatical year during which the fruit belonged to whoever wished to pluck it. Was not this last year of Jesus' ministry the sabbatical year, the year of grace par excellence for Israel?

The olive tree was precious to the people of Galilee. The oil of its fruits provided them with light, enriched and cooked their food, eased their aching muscles, soothed the pain of their wounds, and gave the finishing touch to their grooming. When Jesus sent his disciples to heal the sick, he instructed them to anoint the sick with oil. Mary did the same when he had hurt himself as a child. And the Good Samaritan used oil to dress the wounds of the unfortunate man who had fallen into the robbers' hands. Similarly, Mary used saliva to cure the scratches the child suffered when he fell; like other people of her time, she believed saliva was a good disinfectant. Jesus also used his saliva when he loosened the tongue of the deaf-mute and cured the blind man. Mark was the only evangelist who dared to record a gesture so surprising—for Jesus could cure with one single word, and at a distance—yet so profoundly human.[65]

With the olive tree and the fig tree, the vineyard was part of the Palestinian landscape. It was so identified with it that it had become the very symbol of Israel and the Promised Land. "The vineyard of the Lord of hosts / is the house of Israel," as the song of the vineyard in Isaiah proclaims.[66] In the Temple, one could admire, above the portal between the vestibule and what was called the Holy, an immense vine of gold with clusters of grapes all made of gold and, according to Flavius Josephus, as tall as a human being.[67] Jesus was able to declare that he himself was the true vine and that no one could enter the spiritual temple and find the Father except by passing through him.[68]

The child Jesus may well have witnessed the planting of a new vineyard. After having removed the stones from a field, people surrounded it with a fence, dug out a wine press, even built a tower

65. Mark 6:13; 7:33; 8:23; Luke 10:34. The cures of the Canaanite woman's daughter (Matt 15:21-28) and of son of the royal official in Capernaum (John 4:46-54) are worked at a distance and by words only.

66. Isa 5:7.

67. Flavius Josephus, *De Bello Judaico*, bk. 5, 5:4. See Flavius Josephus, *De Bello Judaico*, vol. 2:1 (München: Kösel, 1963) 138.

68. John 15:1; 14:6.

there.[69] The way vines are pruned might be surprising to those unfamiliar with vine growing. It would be logical to think that, after
pruning out the dead branches, vinedressers would spare the living branches, those in which the flow of the sap is perceptible and
which will surely bear bunches of grapes. But this is not at all what
vinedressers do. Of course, they cut out the dead branches. But they
do not spare the green ones either; they cut them out or back as
well. Vinedressers explain that this is how they increase the yield.

Later on, Jesus remembered how the vines were pruned. The
vinegrower was the heavenly Father.

> He removes every branch in me that bears no fruit. Every branch
> that bears fruit he prunes.[70]

## The Galilean Landscape

The Galilean landscape was the book in which, as a child, Jesus
learned to read God's name. He looked directly into what he himself called "the face of earth and sky" (JB). When the sky was fire
red in the evening, people said, "It will be fair weather." And when
the dawn was fire red and threatening, people said, "It will be stormy
today." "You know how to interpret the appearance of earth and
sky," Jesus said. "Why can you not read 'the signs of the times' and
recognize that the messianic days have come?"[71]

Jesus walked in creation as in the garden of God. He spoke to
the barren fig tree as if he were addressing a person.[72] Likewise,
he "rebuked" the unleashed storm which was harrying the apostles' boat on the lake. He said to the sea, "Peace! Be still!" It is the
same word, "be muzzled," he had addressed to the unclean spirit
that shouted in the synagogue of Capernaum.[73]

Jesus went to the synagogue "as was his custom."[74] One naturally surmises that he joined in the community's prayer. But the

69. Matt 21:33; Mark 12:1, quoting Isa 5:2.
70. John 15:2. The image of the vine is also used in the parable of the wicked tenants,
according to Matt 21:33-46; Mark 12:1-12; Luke 20:9-19.
71. Matt 16:2-3. Tradition hesitates on the authenticity of this text. But Luke 12:54-56
has an equivalent parallel.
72. Matt 21:18-19; Mark 11:12-14. Luke's tradition did not keep this episode and
replaced it with the fig tree which is given another chance after three years of barren-
ness (Luke 13:6-9).
73. Mark 4:38; 1:25.
74. Luke 4:16.

Gospels do not speak of this prayer in common. On the other hand, they like to mention his solitary prayer, especially on "the mountain by himself."[75] Sometimes, he even "spent the night in prayer to God."[76] Sometimes too, he got up long before dawn in order to withdraw alone to a desert place to pray.[77]

It has been noted that Jesus loved mountains. They mark some of the most important hours of his messianic ministry. Thus, we can cite the mountain of the temptation, where he gained the upper hand over Satan; the mountain of the Beatitudes, the pulpit from where he promulgated the new law; the mountain where he chose the Twelve; the mountain where he miraculously multiplied the loaves; the mountain of the transfiguration; and after his resurrection, the mountain from which he sent his disciples on their universal mission; and finally, the mountain of the ascension.[78] In all, seven mountains—a good number. Is it appropriate to see this number as theologically significant?

In fact, we are ignorant of the precise motives for Jesus' preference for mountains, especially as places for solitary prayer. It has been thought that he loved to place himself within the tradition of the Old Testament, where mountains—particularly Sinai—were the places of revelation and worship. Maybe. It has also been noted that, with the exception of the Mount of Olives, no mountain is mentioned by name, as if Jesus had wanted to avoid making any one mountain especially holy. In any case, what is certain is that mountains offered him a place of peace and silence far from the tumultuous agitation of the crowds. Thus, when people wanted to make him king, after the multiplication of the loaves, "he withdrew again to the mountain by himself."[79] But it is also certain that Jesus loved this intimacy with nature where he felt close to God.

Never was anyone more a child of God than he. Never was any child of God closer to creation. No religion is more spiritual than the one he announced; no religion transcends to the same degree

75. Matt 14:23; see Mark 6:46.

76. Luke 6:12.

77. Luke 5:16. See also Luke 19:18. Jesus' prayer is a theme in Luke's tradition. See Deiss, *Synopse*, 347.

78. Matt 4:8; 5:1; Mark 3:13; Luke 6:12; Matt 15:29; 17:1; Mark 9:2; Luke 9:28; Matt 28:17; Acts 1:12. V. Mora, *La symbolique de la création*, Lectio divina 114 (Paris: Cerf, 1981) underlines the importance of the seven mountains in Matthew's Gospel; he stresses that of the "mountain" of Golgotha.

79. John 6:15.

earthly realities, even the most precious ones; no religion is written more intimately in the innermost recesses of the human heart.
But, at the same time, no religion seems closer to earthly realities.
In the gospel of Jesus, there is no exposition of sublime theology,
no sapiential discourse similar to what almost all ancient religions
produced (for instance, to name only two, the mystical treasures
of India and China). Only very simple realities: a mustard seed in
Joseph's hand, a little yeast in Mary's hand, a hen and her chicks,
the sparrows, the doves and the young ravens, the children play-
ing in the street, the clouds moving across the sky, the evening breeze
tempering the fire of the day, the lilies of the field in their bright
colors, the growing wheat, the weeds in the furrows, the sheep and
goats and wolves, the vine and the fig tree, the oil which soothes
the pain caused by wounds, the mountains which offer a refuge for
prayer—in brief, the whole of the Galilean countryside arises before us in its majestic simplicity, seems to speak to us, and through
Jesus' mouth, teaches us the reign of God.

Mark observes that when Jesus proclaimed the "mysteries of the
kingdom,"

> with many such parables he spoke the word to them, as they were
> able to hear it; he did not speak to them except in parables, but he
> explained everything in private to his disciples.[80]

Jesus' universe was a universe of signs which reveal God. Not
like a mirror which reflects God's face, but rather like an icon which
invites us to go deeper into God's mystery.

### Creation, Sign of God

The Galilean countryside is rich in its variety of plants and
animals.[81] What the Gospels reflect of this countryside and what
we have considered represents only a minuscule part of this richness.

But what is absolutely unique in the way Jesus regarded and
admired creation is the religious significance he attributed to it.
Plants and animals are revelations of the Creator. Jesus admired,
not the richness of the Galilean countryside, but the richness of

---

80. Mark 4:33-34; see Matt 13:34.
81. Just as an example, 2,136 species and sub-species of plants have been identified
in Palestine and the region across the Jordan. See Abel, *Géographie*, 204.

meaning which he discovered in the lowliest of creatures. If he was so interested in plants and animals, it was because they spoke to him of the Father who created them. If the landscape of Galilee suggested to him such colorful parables, it was because he saw the memory of God dwelling in it. If he so admired the lilies of the fields and the birds of the sky, it was because he venerated the Providence of the Father in them. To contemplate "the face of earth and sky" (JB)[82] was, for Jesus, to admire the features of the Father's face.

From whom did Jesus acquire this vision of God in creation? From the religious environment in which he lived, of course, that is, from his familiarity with the Hebrew Scriptures and from his roots in the tradition of Israel, but also, it is fitting to add, from his parents. His first teachers in the art of using parables were Joseph and Mary. And his first school of religious formation was his home in Nazareth.

That Jesus led an exemplary life is obvious to all Christians. We are all invited to admire creation with Jesus' eyes, as it were, to read in it the signs of God, to discover in it paths to heaven. Through the teaching they gave to Jesus, Joseph and Mary continue to teach us even today.

82. Luke 12:56.

# Chapter 4

# Jesus in the Temple, His Father's House

The first words Jesus pronounced, like those of all the children in the world, were addressed to his father and mother: *Abba* (Daddy) and *Imma* (Mommy). And the first words the Gospels have preserved for us concern his heavenly Father, "I must be in my Father's house."

Like a solemn postlude, this appealing and mysterious story of Jesus in the Temple concludes Luke's cycle of infancy narratives. Jesus is still called "child" (*pais*, Luke 2:43, or *teknon*, 2:48, which is a term of endearment). The source of the account is certainly Mary's "memoirs." Luke writes, "His mother treasured all these things [*rhemata*] in her heart."[1] But we do not know by what route the story made its way into Luke's text.[2] Some commentators wonder whether the story was added later to the preceding narratives, therefore at another redactional level. Indeed, Joseph is presented here as Jesus' father in the same way Mary is said to be his mother. And nothing is said about the virginal conception as described in

---

1. Luke 2:51. *Rhema* translates the Hebrew *dabar* and can mean now "word," "discourse," now "event," "history," "thing." Thus in Gen 15:1, where the Septuagint translates after these *rhemata*, we must understand, not "after these words," but "after these events." According to biblical thinking, "history is the event expressed and narrated in the word . . . word and thing are equivalent" (Procksch, *ThWNT*, 4:91-92).

2. Luke has left his mark on the original text. His literary mannerisms prove this, especially the grouping of two terms, a device of which he is fond. One can cite, "relatives and friends" (2:44), "listening to them and asking them questions" (2:46), "his understanding and his answers" (2:47), "divine and human favor" (2:52).

the story of the Annunciation. Further on, in Jesus' genealogy, Luke carefully notes that Joseph was, "(as was thought)" Jesus' father.[3]

## The Pilgrimage to Jerusalem

The Law recorded in Deuteronomy (16:16) prescribed three yearly pilgrimages to Jerusalem:

> Three times a year all your males shall appear before the LORD your God at the place that he will choose: at the festival of unleavened bread, at the festival of weeks, and at the festival of booths. They shall not appear before the LORD empty-handed.

We do not know exactly how closely the Jews observed this law in Jesus' time. The Holy Family, so careful to observe "everything required by the law of the Lord,"[4] probably made the three yearly pilgrimages. We may reasonably assume that the Palestinian Jews went to Jerusalem at least once a year and those living outside the boundaries of Israel made the journey at least once during their lifetimes.[5]

In fact, the pilgrimage was obligatory only for men. But in devout families, women and children would have chosen to join the male pilgrims.

The age of religious maturity was, and is, between the ages of twelve and thirteen. It was thought that boys reached puberty at thirteen. Therefore, at twelve, Jesus could well have been considered as having become "bar mitzvah" ("son of the Law"), subject to the whole of the Law. Fathers were urged to initiate their children into the observance of the precepts[6] long before they had attained this age. And so it is probable that Joseph had taken Jesus on the Jerusalem pilgrimage long before he had reached the age of twelve. Indeed, it is unlikely that Joseph and Mary, who had prayed with the child,

> How lovely is your dwelling place,
> O LORD of hosts!

---

3. Luke 3:23.
4. Luke 2:39.
5. J. Jeremias, *Jérusalem au temps de Jésus* (Paris: Cerf, 1967) 114.
6. Strack-Billerbeck, 2:144-45.

> My soul longs, indeed it faints
> for the courts of the LORD,[7]

would have left for Jerusalem, leaving the child home.

It is against this background of religious traditions that Luke sets his story. Here is a literal translation of the Greek text (itself a copy of the original Hebrew or Aramaic) in order to show that Luke did not compose this passage, but simply reproduced his source.

> *2:41* And his parents went each year to Jerusalem for the festival of the Passover.   *42* And when he was twelve years old, they went up as usual for the festival.   *43* And when at the end of the festival they started to return, the boy Jesus stayed behind in Jerusalem. And his parents did not know it.   *44* Now, assuming that he was in the group of travelers, they went a day's journey. And they looked for him among their relatives and friends.   *45* And when they did not find him, they returned to Jerusalem to search for him.

Passover festivities last seven days. Jesus seems to have enjoyed a certain freedom throughout this festive week. In spite of the mystery that surrounded his origin, Jesus was like any child his age, already asserting a certain autonomy as do all children entering adolescence. His parents assumed that he fully participated in all aspects of the feast. The flood of pilgrims was enormous: in Jesus' day, Jerusalem had about twenty thousand inhabitants (within the city walls), but the number of pilgrims could be in the neighborhood of one hundred thousand.[8] A twelve-year-old child can easily be lost sight of in the hubbub of a festive pilgrimage. When returning to Nazareth, his parents assumed he was "in the group of travelers . . . among their relatives and friends."

In what follows, our attention is drawn in two directions: we have a story we could call "Jesus among the Teachers," and another we could title "Jesus in His Father's House."

### Jesus among the Teachers

> *2:46* And after three days they found him in the temple, sitting among the teachers and listening to them and asking them questions.

7. Ps 84:1-2.
8. According to Jeremias' calculations in *Jérusalem*, 121-24.

47 And all who heard him were amazed at his understanding and his answers.

Sometimes, people have thought that the three days of search and anguish were an allusion to the three days that separated Jesus' death from Easter morning and somehow foreshadowed the paschal mystery. But the formula of the primitive kerygma, as proclaimed in the early community, states that Jesus rose "on the third day"[9] and not "after three days," as is said here. It is natural to divide these three days into one day on the way back to Nazareth, one day to return to Jerusalem, and one day of search.

How are we to understand "they found him in the temple, sitting among the teachers"? Must we imagine the romantic scene, the subject of so many paintings, where the child Jesus, represented as a curly-headed young boy sitting on a throne, is charming the old teachers swooning away with admiration before him? Or must we understand more simply that Jesus had become the teachers' student? In other words, does Jesus appear as a master or as a disciple, as teaching or as taught?

The second hypothesis seems more plausible and closer to historic fact.

But it is probable that after Jesus' resurrection, the Christian community enlarged the original significance of the story. Indeed, biblical tradition was familiar with examples of adolescents promised to a prodigious destiny and who had demonstrated a profound wisdom at an early age.[10] It was believed that when Solomon acceded to the throne and pronounced his celebrated judgment, he was only twelve years old. Likewise, Samuel had begun to prophesy at the age of twelve. Again, Daniel was also supposed to have been twelve years old when he was called to judge Susanna's case. Now, the readers who were familiar with biblical traditions knew that here, in Jesus, there was more than Solomon, Samuel, and Daniel. They were therefore more inclined to admire the wisdom of Jesus' answers than the appropriateness of his questions. Moreover, it was noted that the child was not seated at the feet of the teachers—as a pupil at the master's feet, as later Mary of Bethany at Jesus' feet,

---

9. See Luke 9:22; 18:33; 24:7, 21, 46; see also 13:32. See also Laurentin, *Evangiles de l'enfance*, 101, and the remarks of Brown, *Birth*, 487.

10. See Laurentin, ibid., 147-54; Brown, ibid., 482.

as Paul at Gamaliel's feet[11]—but rather in their midst, *en mesō*, as Daniel among the judges. In any case, Luke stresses that Jesus' listeners "were amazed at his understanding and his answers." Twice, he makes mention of Jesus' wisdom.[12] Such admiration is more understandable if it had for its object the child's intelligence rather than his questions.

Jesus-Wisdom teaching in the Temple, what better fulfillment, in the eyes of the Christian community, of a prophecy in Isaiah's book (2:3).

> Out of Zion shall go forth instruction,
>     and the word of the Lord from Jerusalem.

## Jesus in His Father's House

When Joseph and Mary found Jesus, "they *were astonished.*" Luke uses the same verb to describe the astonishment of the crowd when Jesus began his ministry in Capernaum, "They *were astonished* at his teaching, because he spoke with authority." He also uses the same verb to describe the astonishment of the crowd witnessing Jesus' power when he expelled the demon, "All *were astonished* at the greatness of God."[13]

It is easy to understand the astonishment of the crowd at Jesus' teaching and miracles. But how are we to understand Joseph's and Mary's astonishment? Mary should have been less astonished than anybody. What Gabriel had revealed to her, at the Annunciation, of Jesus' marvelous vocation had remained engraved in her memory and heart. Her question betrays her motherly anguish.

> Child *[teknon]*, why have you treated us like this? Look, your father and I have been searching for you in great anxiety.[14]

*Teknon* ("child") is a term full of tenderness. *Odunōmenoi* ("in great anxiety") is a very strong word. Luke uses this word only once more in his Gospel, in the parable of Lazarus when he speaks of

11. Luke 10:39; Acts 22:3.
12. Luke 2:40, 52.
13. Luke 4:32; 9:43, author's translation.
14. Luke 2:48.

the suffering of the rich man in Hades.[15] Joseph's and Mary's anguish, we could say, was a mortal anguish.

Astonishing, too, is Jesus' answer:

> Why were you searching for me? Did you not know that I must be in my Father's [business/house]?[16]

Was it not natural for parents tormented by anguish to search for their child lost for three days?

But, obviously, Luke's intention is not to report the anecdote—a slight one at that—of a boy lost in the course of a pilgrimage, then found again in the Temple, but rather to present the mystery of Jesus' vocation. The accent of the story falls on the word "father." On the one hand, there is the reproach, *"Your father and I have been searching for you."* On the other, there is the answer, "I must be in *my Father's* house." On the one hand, obedience to the heavenly Father, on the other, submission to the earthly father. On the one hand, filiation according to grace, on the other, filiation according to family ties.

Jesus did not refuse to be obedient to his earthly parents. Luke 2:51 notes,

> Then he went down with them and was obedient to them.

But at the very moment when he was about to leave the Temple, he asserted that obedience to the Father was the supreme rule of his life.

A problem of interpretation remains. Must we understand Jesus' answer to mean "I must be about my Father's business" as most of the older translations[17] did, or as "I must be in my Father's house" as most recent translations do, with minimal variants? Luke's text lacks precision.[18] Literally, one has, "Did you not know that *in the en tois* of my Father I must be?" In the Greek, what does *en tois* refer to?

---

15. Luke 16:24.

16. Luke 2:49.

17. We note the following translations. "About my Father's business": KJV (1611), CCD (1941); "busy with my Father's affairs": JB (1966); "in my Father's house": RSV (1946), NEB (1961), NJB (1985), NAB (1986), NRSV (1989).

18. A. Chouraqui, *La Bible traduite et présentée par A. Chouraqui* (Paris: Desclée de Brouwer, 1985), renders well the lack of precision by translating, "I must be at what is my Father's."

The translation "about my Father's business" is vague enough to render the Greek. Although banal, it rightly indicates that Jesus must dwell within the sphere of his Father's interests.

The translation "in my Father's house" is a good interpretation.[19] However, by being more precise than the Greek, it has the disadvantage of linking Jesus' activity to the Temple, of sacralizing the very place of which Luke writes, "The Most High does not dwell in houses made with human hands,"[20] and whose destruction Jesus himself announced.[21] In any case, Jesus' piety does not seem all that attached to the Temple. Of course, on the occasion of the pilgrimages, he taught there every day,[22] sometimes in the portico of Solomon,[23] where even pagans had access and could listen to his words. He proclaimed that the Temple was "a house of prayer for all the nations."[24] And one can reasonably assume that he joined in the prayer of the community. But the Gospels do not explicitly mention that he ever prayed there or had sacrifices offered in his name.[25] Therefore, there is little interest in linking Jesus too closely to the Temple.

The translation "in my Father's house" is a felicitous rendition of the Greek, provided we understand it as meaning more than residing in a building consecrated to God. This translation also includes, but is not limited to, attending to the Father's business. To be in the Father's house "is to place oneself at the very heart of the filial condition, of the knowledge and revelation of the Father."[26] Some priests, scribes, and Pharisees might have been staying in the Father's house; but they were not dwelling with the Father. The Temple merchants who sold the victims intended for the sacrifices might have been busy with God's business, and yet neither did they dwell with the Father. On the contrary, Jesus, even when crisscrossing the Galilean countryside far away from the Temple, was dwelling with his Father. His own house of prayer, in the solitude of the moun-

---

19. See the excellent dossier presented by Laurentin, *Evangiles de l'enfance*, 56–72.

20. Acts 7:48. Luke records Stephen's discourse before the Sanhedrin.

21. John 2:19.

22. Matt 26:55; Mark 14:49; Luke 22:53. On Luke's traditions favorable to the Temple, see Deiss, *Synopse*, 349.

23. John 10:23.

24. Mark 11:17.

25. According to Charlier, *Jésus*, 98.

26. H. Legrand, *A cause de l'Evangile*, Lectio Divina 123 (Paris: Cerf, 1985) 424.

tains, was his heart, full of praise and love for the Father. The only temple where he had to reside forever was the holy will of his Father.

## The Father's Call

Pondering the importance of the Temple and the mystery of Jesus, the Christian community declared, "Something greater than the temple is here."[27] Pondering the story of Jesus in the Temple, can we likewise say, "Something more than the necessity of being in the Father's house is expressed here"? Can we enter more deeply into the heart of the story and decode its meaning in the history of Jesus' vocation?

Two questions seem to structure the text: Mary's question, "Child, why have you treated us like this?" and Jesus' question, "Why were you searching for me?" These two questions collide head-on, hiding a mystery in which we cannot enter.

Here we have a twelve-year-old boy, full of wisdom and on whom divine favor rested.[28] Would that he had received the wisdom—and also the simplicity—to warn his parents of what he planned to do! Could he have not been aware of the mortal anguish he was going to cause them? Was it possible that he premeditated, so to speak, his parents' anguish? What normal child would do this? And would Jesus do it? Therefore, if he did not forewarn his parents, it was because he had in no way anticipated when he joined the pilgrimage that he would remain in Jerusalem unbeknownst to his parents. And if he behaved in this manner, it was because he was moved by an inner necessity. Consequently, besides the parents and Jesus, there must have been a third person who dominated and directed the event.

This person was the Father. It was the Father alone, the Master of history, who ordained and directed Jesus' life, always according to loving designs. As in a prophetic calling, the Father revealed God's very self to the child in a totally unexpected manner. Long ago, God had surprised Moses when he was leading the sheep of his father-in-law, Jethro, to pasture at Mount Horeb and had established him as shepherd of the people for the Exodus. God had seized

27. Matt 12:6.
28. Luke 2:40, 52.

Amos following his flock and tending his sycamore trees. God had grasped Isaiah, who protested that his lips were unclean, and had thrown him into a hurricane of glory. God had swooped down upon Ezekiel on the banks of the river Chebar, among the exiles in Babylon, and had opened the skies before his eyes.[29] Similarly, the Father had burst into Jesus' consciousness and had enjoined upon him the necessity of remaining in God's house, in God's service.

We do not know how the Father revealed this inner necessity to the child (it could have been an interior grace, as with the prophets of old). But we know with certainty that it happened.

Indeed, Jesus said, "I must be in my Father's house." Now, the phrase *dei einai me* ("I must be"), or its equivalent, is characteristic of Luke's language. This well-known *dei* ("one must," "it is necessary") expresses the sovereign will of God. Luke uses it when speaking either of the necessity of fulfilling the Scriptures[30] or of the necessity of the passion and the resurrection according to the Scriptures[31] or, lastly, of the necessity of proclaiming the good news, a necessity also deriving from the Scriptures.[32]

When he declared, "I must be in my Father's house," Jesus did not express a decision that he would have taken by himself, but the will of God resting upon him. This first *dei* ("I must") in Luke's Gospel, this first word of Jesus, announced his total obedience to the Father. It would lead him from his adolescence through the sufferings of his passion into the light of the resurrection. Then, he would dwell forever in the heavenly temple with his Father.

How did Joseph and Mary enter into this mystery of Jesus' life? How did they live it? We do know that Mary "treasured all these things in her heart."[33] Later on she might have concluded that, with Joseph, she herself had been the cause of Jesus' way of acting. Had not she, the servant of the Lord, and Joseph, the obedient one, taught their child absolute obedience to the Father, the supreme necessity of living constantly in God's will? Was not their daily life a dwelling with the Father? It was indeed in the intimacy of an earthly fam-

29. Exod 3:1-2; Amos 7:14-15; Isa 6:4-5; Ezek 1:1.

30. Luke 24:44; see also 22:37.

31. Luke 24:7; see also Luke 9:22 (the only text that Luke has in common with Matt 16:21 and Mark 8:31); Luke 17:25; 24:26.

32. Luke 4:43.

33. Luke 2:51.

ily that Joseph and Mary had taught the child to prefer intimacy with the heavenly Father to any human love.

And this intimacy with God did not impair the unity of their family. Rather, it gathered the three of them close to the Father.


### The Song of Faith

At the end of his narrative, Luke faithfully reproduces his source as is shown by the six sentences placed in juxtaposition.

> And they did not understand what he said to
>   them.
> And he went down with them.
> And he came to Nazareth.
> And he was obedient to them.
> And his mother treasured all these things
>   [*rhemata*] in her heart.
> And Jesus increased in wisdom and in years,
>   and in divine and human favor.


### *The Pilgrimage of Faith*

We know Mary's faith: she is proclaimed blessed precisely for having believed. We also known the humble submission of Joseph's faith to God's will: he was obedient love. Here, we learn that so perfectly obedient a faith can coexist with anguish of soul, "Look, your father and I have been searching for you in great anxiety."

We also learn that so submissive a faith can dwell in the land of darkness, "They did not understand what he said to them."

There is no indication that Joseph and Mary, as they progressed on the road of their lives, sought to guess in advance what God's plan was for them and their child. With each new dawn, they simply walked on the path that God placed before them. Speaking of Mary, Vatican II rightly says, "She progressed in her faith pilgrimage."[34] We may add to this teaching of Vatican II by saying, "She progressed by walking hand in hand with Joseph in their faith pilgrimage."

---

34. Constitution on the Church, *Lumen Gentium*, 58. On Mary's faith, see Laurentin, *Evangiles de l'enfance*, 174–77, and the dossiers concerning this tradition, pp. 189–234.

### The Law of Growth

Popular legends love to embroider on the theme of the marvelous precocity of their heroes' intelligence.[35] Such was the case for Buddha in India, Cyrus in Persia, Alexander the Great, Augustus (when still in his cradle!). Apocryphal writings did not always know how to resist the temptation to embellish their stories by attributing to Jesus a stupefying intellectual precocity. The Arab Gospel of the infancy tells of a teacher of the Law who asked Jesus, when he was in the Temple, whether he had read the Holy Scriptures. Jesus is supposed to have answered:

> [I have read] the books and the contents of the Law, the explanation of these books, of the Torah, of the commandments, of the laws and mysteries which are in the prophets' books, all things inaccessible to the reason of any creature.

And the teacher said:

> As for me, up to now, I have not attained such a knowledge, and neither have I heard of such a knowledge. What do you think will become of this child?[36]

There is nothing like this in Luke's story. On the contrary, Jesus' humble submission to the law of growth is marvelous.

> Jesus increased in wisdom and in years, and in divine and human favor.

This sentence, moving in its humility, concludes the infancy narratives. To the growth of Mary's faith corresponded the growth of "wisdom" in Jesus, this wisdom which led him to discover his Father's will day after day.

Of course, Jesus possibly received, like the prophets of old, particular revelations which showed him the path of his future mission. But the Gospels say nothing of the sort. Eighteen years after his call at the age of twelve to be a familiar resident in the Father's house, Jesus received at his baptism his investiture as Servant and Son of God. Concerning this Servant, it is said that the Lord "morning by morning wakens [his] ear" so that he may obey God's voice.[37]

35. See Laurentin, ibid., 147–52.
36. Quoted by Laurentin, ibid., 153.
37. Isa 50:4-5.

Concerning this Son, it is said that "he learned obedience" (*hupakoē*, literally "he listened with bent head") from his sufferings.[38] Thus, the way was mapped out from Jesus' first word to his last word on the cross. It was the daily discovery of and filial obedience to the Father's holy will.

*Toward the Father's House*

The Book of Isaiah describes the jubilation of pilgrims when they set out for Jerusalem:

> You shall have a song as in the night when a holy festival is kept; and gladness of heart, as when one sets out to the sound of the flute to go to the mountain of the LORD, to the Rock of Israel.[39]

The Holy Family knew the intoxication of the feast, this joy which transfigured the heart when one departed for "the house of God, / with glad shouts and songs of thanksgiving, / a multitude keeping festival."[40] Even Jesus immersed himself in the feast. Certainly, it is not a matter of profound theological reflection but simply of human truth to imagine that the one whom Gabriel had proclaimed the Son of the Most High sang and prayed with the others in his caravan; laughed and played with the boys and girls his age; danced to the sound of flutes, tambourines, and lyres; was swept off his feet upon suddenly discovering, in all its glittering splendor, the Father's house.

> We ponder your steadfast love, O God,
>     in the midst of your temple.
> Your name, O God, like your praise,
>     reaches to the ends of the earth.[41]

Jesus lived the essence of this pilgrimage joy. For this essence was not to journey toward the Temple but to come near to the Lord with all one's heart and then dwell for ever with the Father.

38. Heb 5:8.
39. Isa 30:29.
40. Ps 42:4.
41. Ps 48:9-10.

# Chapter 5
# Jesus' Humanity

As a child, Jesus grew up between Joseph and Mary, at the very center of their love. We have no information whatsoever concerning the expression of this love. We may suppose that they exchanged the tender words that all lovers on earth have said to each other since the dawn of humankind and that they rendered each other services which are the daily expressions of love. It is in this environment of human tenderness, enhanced by heavenly grace, that the child grew up, that he discovered his fraternal relation with men and women which he transformed into love for God. A calm and tender equilibrium, a perfectly mastered sexuality, a peaceful acceptance of feminine friendships were obvious in him when he reached maturity. What is this explanation? These traits were rooted in the home of Nazareth. His "humanization" and his masculinity had been formed by his closeness to Joseph and Mary.

Here as elsewhere—as is the case for any human being—it is impossible to estimate what is to be attributed respectively to nature and to grace, as well as to the formation he received from his parents. But this last element cannot be ignored.

## "MOVED WITH PITY"

Jesus' heart, like Mary's,[1] was a humble and gentle heart. It was also an extremely strong heart since Jesus dared to confront the en-

1. See pp. 62–64.

tire world and its wickedness with the power of his love as his sole weapon. We learn from the Gospels that it was also a tender and compassionate heart, particularly sensitive to misfortune and poverty. To express this vulnerability of Jesus' heart, the Gospels use the verb *splagchnizesthai* which literally means "to be moved in one's innermost core." This verb is extremely important in the theology of the incarnation. In biblical vocabulary, *splagchna* ("the guts") designate in human beings "what is most intimate and hidden . . . what today we call the heart."[2] Thus, when Joseph saw his brothers again after they had come to Egypt, "he was overcome with affection for his brother [Benjamin], and he was about to weep. So he went into a private room and wept there."[3] Paul writes to his Philippians, "I long for all of you with the compassion of Christ Jesus," that is in the heart of Christ.[4] In the short letter to Philemon, he intercedes for Onesimus who is, he says, as "my own heart."[5] Generally, the image of the entrails is associated with the idea of compassion. Then, one speaks of "feelings of tender compassion"[6] or else of "tender mercy of our God."[7] When Matthew writes in 9:36 that Jesus *esplagchnisthē*, we must understand that he was moved in the deepest parts of his being, in his guts; that his heart heaved; that it beat faster; that it fluttered with pity and compassion.

The Synoptic tradition seems hesitant, even embarrassed, when it comes to recording this profoundly human emotion that shook Jesus down to his entrails, as if it feared to overemphasize his humanity, to detract from his messianic dignity. But this sensibility of Jesus incontestably belongs to the most primitive levels of the Synoptic tradition.

Thus, Mark, and he alone, notes that Jesus was *moved with pity* when he suddenly saw before him, in the midst of the crowd, a leper who entreated him, "If you choose, you can make me clean." Luke observes that the unfortunate man was "covered with leprosy." Jesus stretched out his hand, touched the man covered with leprosy, and healed him. Matthew and Luke faithfully follow Mark in their

2. Spicq, *Notes de lexicographie,* 3:812–13.
3. Gen 43:30. When the word is used in the singular, *splagchnos* (*rehen* in Hebrew) means "womb."
4. Phil 1:8.
5. Phlm 12.
6. Col 3:12 (BJ).
7. Luke 1:78.

recounting of the miracle, but they erase from their texts Jesus' visceral emotion.[8]

Both Mark and Matthew relate that Jesus was *moved with pity* when he saw the large crowd which was "like sheep without a shepherd." Mark adds that Jesus began to teach them at length. It is from this pity that the first multiplication of the loaves flowed as from its wellspring. Luke knows this narrative but says nothing about Jesus' emotion.[9]

Before the second multiplication of the loaves, Jesus himself revealed his emotion. He declared, "I have compassion *[splagchnizomai]* for the crowd, because they have been with me now for three days and have nothing to eat."[10] Luke does not have a second account of the multiplication of the loaves.

Finally, only Matthew tells us that Jesus was *moved with compassion* when two blind men came near and implored his pity. Jesus touched their eyes, and they regained their sight.[11] Neither Mark nor Luke mentions Jesus' emotion.

In the threefold Synoptic tradition, Luke systematically omits speaking of the emotion that moved Jesus' heart. On the other hand, in his own tradition, he keeps the verb *splagchnizesthai* as he found it in the story of the raising of the son of the widow of Nain.[12] This is a story of singular beauty in Luke's tradition. On the road which goes down from the town of Nain, near the city gate, Jesus met a funeral procession. A widow was weeping: the biblical image of despondency. She was weeping over her only son: the biblical image of utter bereavement. "With her was a large crowd from the town" to support her in her grief. Who would not empathize with this unmitigated sorrow? What was Jesus going to do? Say the conventional trite words? "You have my sincere sympathy. Courage. God will see to your needs." Or else pious words? "Do not worry about the morrow. Sufficient to the day is the burden thereof (as I taught you in the Sermon on the Mount").[13] At first, Jesus did

8. Compare Mark 1:40-41 with Matt 8:1-3 and Luke 5:12-13.
9. Compare Mark 6:34 with Matt 9:35-36 and 14:13-14 (we probably have doublets here) and Luke 9:11.
10. Mark 8:2; Matt 15:32.
11. Compare Matt 20:33-34 (9:27-30 is probably a doublet) with Mark 10:51-52 and Luke 18:41-43.
12. Luke 7:11-17.
13. Matt 6:34.

not say a word. Even before saying to the widow, "Do not weep," his heart was broken; his innermost core shuddered; *"he had compassion* for her."[14] He touched the bier, raised the dead man, and gave him back to his mother. The crowd glorified God for this admirable miracle. But Jesus' heart was even more admirable.

John's tradition does not use the verb *splagchnizesthai.* But as shown by John, Jesus' heart was as vulnerable as in the Synoptics: he cried at the tomb of his friend Lazarus. Seeing the tears of Lazarus' sister Mary, and those of the friends who had come from Jerusalem to console her, "he was greatly disturbed in spirit and deeply moved. . . . He began to weep."[15] There is no place in the Gospels for a solemnly impassive Messiah. Jesus does not stifle his tears in the presence of a woman he loved.

What shall we conclude? Was Mary—with Joseph, of course— the source of the sensibility of Jesus' heart?

What counts is not the fact that a heart be more or less emotional and vulnerable, but the nature of the motives which move the heart and arouse pity. Now, Jesus is said to have been moved with pity before the imploring distress of the leper "covered with leprosy"; before the sad fate of the crowd abandoned to itself and without a shepherd to guide it, without a master to instruct it; before the hunger of those who had followed him for three days and were in danger of fainting on the way; before the misery of the two blind men begging him to cure them; before the tears of the widow of Nain wailing over her only son. Clearly, the community which moved Jesus was that of the Beatitudes; that of the poor of all sorts, of the hungry, of those who weep. It was the same community which, in the Magnificat, was filled with God's mercy.

In order to show without a doubt that he was in unity with that community, Jesus touched the leper without worrying about contracting an impurity (according to Jewish law). He touched the eyes of the two blind men, touched also the bier of the widow's son in Nain (again contracting a legal impurity). The crowds understood the vulnerability of Jesus' heart. The father of the epileptic boy implored his son's cure in these words, *"Have pity* on us and help us."[16]

---

14. Luke 7:13.
15. John 11:33-35, 38.
16. Mark 9:22.

May we speak of the vulnerability of God's very heart, of God's entrails? James' letter dares to declare, "The Lord is *polysphagchnos* [literally "rich in entrails," that is, in pity] and merciful."[17] The vulnerability of Jesus' heart imitated that of God's heart. And whoever wants to enter the reign must imitate Jesus' heart. This is what the Good Samaritan did. When he saw the unfortunate man who had fallen into the robbers' hands, "he *was moved with pity*." Jesus concluded the parable by saying to us, "Go and do likewise."[18]

17. Jas 5:11, referring to Exod 34:6 and Ps 103:8. In the parable of the pitiless debtor, the "lord" (let us understand "God") is also said to be moved with pity, Matt 18:27, whereas the pitiless debtor is condemned for having lacked pity (18:33).
18. Luke 10:33, 37.

## WOMEN ACCOMPANYING JESUS

The attitude Jesus had toward women was new in Israel. From the testimony of the Gospels, we can state that "Jesus was concerned about women as much as, if not more than, he was concerned about men."[1]

This attitude of Jesus was in full harmony with his messianic ministry. Women were of little importance in Jewish circles. But Jesus always sided with the humble, the lowly, therefore with women.

In return, women honored his ministry. They offered their friendship; they welcomed him with faith. Martha's profession of faith at Lazarus' grave, "yes, Lord, I believe that you are the Messiah, the Son of God," is on a par, as far as theological value is concerned, with Peter's at Caesarea Philippi, "you are the Messiah, the Son of the living God."[2] Let us also remember that it was to a woman, Mary Magdalene, Jesus entrusted the first announcement of the resurrection.[3] According to tradition, she was the apostle of the apostles.

### The *Diaconia* of the "Holy Women"

Jesus accepted with utmost simplicity the service of a group of women who provided him with material necessities. He himself was too poor to support himself and at the same time announce the good news. Luke 8:1-3, a passage imitating the style of the Septuagint, relates:

> Soon afterwards, he went on through cities and villages, proclaiming and bringing the good news of the kingdom of God. The twelve were with him, as well as some women who had been cured of evil spirits and infirmities: Mary, called Magdalene, from whom seven demons had gone out, and Joanna, the wife of Herod's steward

---

1. A. Maillot, *Marie, ma soeur* (Paris: Letouzey et Ané, 1990) 98. The author notes that if one adds up all the texts which speak of women, one has the equivalent of 11 or 12 chapters, almost as much text as Mark's Gospel.

2. John 11:27; Matt 16:16.

3. John 20:17.

Chuza, and Susanna, and many others, who provided *[diakonoun]* for them out of their resources.

These women were not a choir of virgins of dazzling virtue, but simply a group of women, of "holy women," as tradition would call them. Several had been freed from "evil spirits" or diseases. Mary Magdalene had been rid of seven demons (in biblical language, diabolical possession does not necessarily mean sexual impurity).

These women had money; Jesus accepted their help with simplicity. They offered their service; he implanted the gospel in their hearts.

In the midst of the discussions, then of the conflicts and hatreds on the part of some Pharisees and scribes, the "holy women" provided Jesus with a haven of peace and friendship. He who, in his evangelizing journeys, lived like a wanderer, like a nestless bird, like a denless fox, who did not have even a stone on which to lay his head,[4] must have blessed his Father for these women's friendship which had been given him and which provided him with rest for both body and heart.

The holy women also assisted him at the foot of the cross. Whereas he was abandoned by all his male disciples, they surrounded him with their presence. Their *diaconia* was therefore not simply a financial support but also a loving presence.

According to the customs of the time, the relations between the sexes were strict. It was known that a rabbi who was careful of his reputation had to abstain from speaking in public with a woman, including his own wife, or his sister or his daughter, for, the saying went, it was not obvious that the woman was his sister or his daughter.[5]

Jesus did not observe these rules of propriety established by the authorities in Israel. He followed his inner law, that which his heart dictated, that which befitted the announcement of the reign. At Jacob's well, he conversed alone with the Samaritan woman. Which certainly did not fail to astonish the disciples. A twofold astonishment. First, because it was a woman—John explicitly points this out: "They were astonished that he was speaking with a woman." Second, because she was a Samaritan—the Samaritan woman herself is surprised by Jesus' boldness: "How is it that you, a Jew, ask

4. Matt 8:20.
5. Strack-Billerbeck, 1:300; 2:438.

a drink of me, a woman of Samaria?"[6] Everybody was nonplussed. Only Jesus seemed perfectly at ease.

The Samaritan woman was no innocent young girl. She had already had five husbands. And the sixth man she was presently living with was not her husband.

This was a dialogue in the light of God. A man and a woman, face to face in their sexual difference, speak as son and daughter of God. Jesus led the woman, who became his sister, into worship "in spirit and truth."[7] This close conversation of children of God counted infinitely more in his eyes than ossified human customs.

We must also note the simplicity with which Jesus accepted the hospitality of Martha and Mary. In 10:38-42, Luke, who records the episode, does not even bother to specify whether Lazarus, their brother, was with them. Through John we learn—it was common knowledge—that "Jesus loved Martha and her sister."[8] And while Martha was working hard over her stove in order to prepare one of Jesus' favorite dishes—what tender-hearted person would not have done the same?—Mary was just sitting at Jesus' feet and drinking in his teaching. With Jesus, the man-woman relationship was not necessarily fraught with ambiguity on the sexual level; it could be illuminated by grace and filled with God's peace, especially when the issue was the discovery that "there is need of only one thing."[9]

### The Loving and Forgiven Sinner

The story of the forgiven and loving sinner, according to Luke 7:36-50, is the supreme revelation of what can be, according to Jesus, the relationship of a man, son of God, with a woman, daughter of God.[10] The relationship of a man with a "sinner" can be ambiguous. He may look at her in order to despise her, to condemn her, to desire her. He may also forgive her. Jesus made of this face to face encounter a love story of perfect limpidity.

---

6. John 4:9, 27.
7. John 4:24.
8. John 11:5.
9. Luke 10:42.
10. This anointing has parallels in the stories of the anointing at Simon the leper's house, in Mark 14:3-9 and Matt 26:6-13, and in the story of the anointing by Mary, Lazarus' sister, in John 12:1-8. The problem of literary convergences does not affect what we are saying here about Luke's account.

We do not know the whole story. Perhaps Luke did not know
it either. Perhaps the sinner had met Jesus before, and he had given
her peace by forgiving her. She then would have come to thank
him for his pardon. She probably had planned on a simple and dig-
nified anointing. But here is what happened: in Jesus' presence, she
was betrayed by her emotion; she was overcome with tenderness
before him. As long as she had lost face, she might as well follow
the bent of her woman's sensibility. All the ingredients of womanly charm, verging on eroticism, are put to use: hair, perfume—an
alabaster jar full of it—kisses. Not a little platonic peck. Luke writes
*katephilei,* which can be rendered by "she covered with kisses"[11] or
"she tenderly kissed" Jesus' feet, washed them with her tears, and
dried them with her hair, this hair which, according to the good
manners of the time, was to be covered with a veil as soon as a
woman went outside the home.

The scene is at the limit of what good manners could tolerate.
What the sinful woman did exceeded, by far, what a married woman
would have done for her husband. Indeed, what wife would dry
her husband's feet with her hair, and especially in public?[12] Jesus
should have stopped her. But he let her do what she did. He was
by no means a man who allowed others to manipulate him. Certain Pharisees whom he called "you brood of vipers"[13] could attest
to that. In the stupefaction that stilled all conversation, Jesus dominated the event. His relationship with the sinful woman was not
a vulnerable relationship of a man with a woman, set on the sexual plane, but the triumphant relationship of the Messiah with a
sinner he befriended, the relationship of the Son of God with a
daughter of God, of the Holy with a woman forgiven, set free. Obviously, this woman retained all her femininity before Jesus' masculinity. Her kisses—"let him kiss me with the kisses of his mouth!"
as the Song of Solomon says—were marks of authentic tenderness,
and her hair—the flowing locks were able to captivate a king —[14]
remained the glory of her womanhood on the feet of the beloved
Master. But all this was driven, with the violence of a new love,

11. Luke 7:38. When the father welcomes the prodigal son home, Luke (15:20) also
writes that he *covered him with kisses (katephilēsen).*

12. This remark is made by Maillot in his excellent analysis of the scene recorded
by Luke 7:36-50, in *Marie, ma soeur,* 26.

13. Matt 23:33.

14. Cant 1:2; 7:6.

onto the shores of another world, a world in which, Paul says, there is in the risen Christ neither man nor woman nor slave nor free.[15] Everything was illuminated by a new light, that of faith and the peace which springs from forgiveness: "Your faith has saved you; go in peace."[16]

The question rises in our hearts: In Jesus, what was the source of such a chastity, so human and so divine? This man, with his perfect beauty, who could have bewitched all women, did not bewitch any. What was the source from which radiated the light that transfigured everything—kisses, hair, perfume—from a markedly sexual act into one of chaste tenderness? And also, to what degree did the education received in his childhood in Nazareth, in his daily contact with Joseph and Mary, influence Jesus' behavior?

Of course, it is impossible to affirm that if parents give the example of a sincere and balanced love, their children will necessarily enjoy a perfect balance on the emotional and sexual planes. It is equally impossible to affirm the contrary. Every life grows and blossoms in its royal freedom before God. In Jesus' case, all we can do is suppose that the perfection of his humanity was rooted, in heavenly grace without any doubt, but also in the perfection of the love of Joseph and Mary.

15. Gal 3:28.
16. Luke 7:50.

## THE MYSTERY OF JESUS' CELIBACY

### Jesus' Chastity and Celibacy

Does the word of Scripture "it is not good that the man should be alone"[1] apply to Jesus, as one might easily think? And how did he live it?

First of all, we should notice that in the Gospels, chastity is not a major theme of his preaching in the announcement of the reign.[2] And the words that express it hardly appear in his vocabulary. Jesus never uses the word "chastity" *(hagneia)*. The word appears elsewhere in the New Testament,[3] but never in the Gospels.

Similarly, Jesus never speaks of "continence" *(egkrateia)*, never uses either the adjective "continent" or the verb "be continent." These words appear elsewhere in the New Testament. If Jesus pronounced them, the Gospels have not recorded them.

Jesus speaks only once of "impurity" *(akatharsia)* when he declares that certain Pharisees, whitewashed tombs, are filled with filth.[4] As to the adjective "unclean," which occurs nineteen times in the Synoptics, it is found only in the expression "unclean spirit." Neither noun nor adjective directly implies any sexual connotation.

The adjective "pure" *(katharos)* can be understood in relation to sexual purity, but is never so used by Jesus. The Beatitude of the pure in heart, according to Matthew 5:8, is inspired by Psalm 24:4. To the question, "Who shall ascend the hill of the LORD? / And who shall stand in his holy place?" the psalm answers, "Those who have clean hands" (that is, who act in an innocent manner) "and pure hearts" (that is, whose intentions are pure).

In the Gospels, Jesus uses the word "unchastity," "fornication" *(porneia)* and the Greek verb meaning "commit adultery" only in the discussion on the indissolubility of marriage and in the list of foul deeds that can come out of the human heart.[5] He mentions

1. Gen 2:18.
2. See J. Guillet, "La chasteté de Jésus-Christ," *Les ambassadeurs du Christ,* ed. P. Rolland, Lire la Bible 92 (Paris: Cerf, 1991) 126–27. This article greatly helped us in our study.
3. For instance, in the pastoral letters, such as Tim 4:12; 5:2.
4. Matt 23:27.
5. "Unchastity" or "fornication," *porneia* in Matt 5:32; 15:19 (cf. Mark 7:21); 19:9. "To commit adultery" translates the verbs *moichasthai* in Matt 5:32; 19:9; Mark 10:11-12, and *moicheuein* in Matt 5:27, 28, 32; 19:18; Mark 10:19; Luke 16:18; 18:20.

prostitutes only twice, the first time to say that they would enter the reign ahead of the so-called just ones because they have been converted to the gospel[6] and a second time in the parable of the prodigal son. This second case is especially significant: the prodigal son lived, according to Jesus, *asōtōs* (literally, "not working his salvation"). But the elder son specified, according to the parable, that he lived with prostitutes.[7] Jesus' vocabulary, it is plain to see, manifests an extreme reserve.

Let us observe that Paul presents an unvarnished vocabulary, which must have been that of his time. He speaks of "fornicators" *(pornoi)*, of "male prostitutes" *(malakoi)*, of "sodomites" *(arsenokoitai)*,[8] of those who commit "shameless acts with men."[9] As a child, Jesus must not have been accustomed to such language in Joseph's and Mary's home. And we find nothing of this nature in his mouth.

These remarks regarding vocabulary allow us to make a first observation. Certain Pharisees brought many accusations against Jesus: he was a glutton, a drunkard; he violated the Sabbath, spoke against the Temple, ate with sinners, went to preach to the Samaritans, had not studied (in *their* schools!), did not keep the devotional fasts. . . . But never did they dare express any doubt concerning his perfect chastity, although he was known to have several women friends. We must therefore suppose that his chastity was so radiant and shone with such clarity that it did not lay itself open to the slightest suspicion.

Here is a second observation: Jesus never gave his chastity as an example. He commended certain virtues that he practiced, like his meekness and humility of heart or his love shown in mutual service.[10]

Celibacy was not a completely inconceivable way of life in Judaism during Jesus' time. It was practiced in Qumran, principally for reasons of ritual purity.[11] But Jesus never made much of this kind of purity.

6. Matt 21:31-32.
7. Luke 15:13, 30.
8. 1 Cor 6:9.
9. Rom 1:27.
10. Matt 11:29; John 13:34; 15:12.
11. P. Grelot, *Introduction à la Bible: Le Nouveau Testament*, vol.6 (Paris: Desclée, 1986) 219.

Often the saying of Jesus in Matthew 19:10-12, on those who "have made themselves eunuchs for the sake of the kingdom of heaven," is presented as an invitation to celibacy. This "numerical saying," in the style of ancient proverbs in three sentences, may have had an independent existence before being attached to the question of the indissolubility of marriage in Matthew 19:1-9. It is extremely violent since it compares celibacy to a mutilation, more precisely a castration. What does it say exactly? Jesus simply states that there are three categories of eunuchs: those who were born that way; those who were made eunuchs by human beings; those who made themselves such for the sake of the reign. It is difficult to see in these sentences an explicit invitation to celibacy. When Jesus uttered an invitation to follow him, he was in the habit of speaking very clearly. For example, he said, *"If you wish to be perfect,* go, sell your possessions, and give the money to the poor . . . then come, follow me."[12] He does not use a formula as mysterious as "let anyone accept this who can." Of course, we must place Jesus' word in the religious context of the time. Certain Pharisees probably reproached Jesus with not being married because in Judaism marriage and procreation were regarded as a religious obligation, therefore a duty for the reign.[13] Jesus claimed for himself the freedom to choose celibacy "for the sake of the kingdom of heaven." This choice is one of the mysteries of his life; it belongs to the domain of God's grace. "Those to whom it is given" can understand this mystery, that is, those who have received from the Father the grace of knowing "the secrets of the kingdom of heaven."[14]

It is only fair to add that the preceding remarks on Jesus' chastity do not exhaust the subject. On the one hand, the Gospels did not transmit to us the totality of Jesus' teaching, but only what they deemed necessary. On the other hand, his teaching on chastity was principally his own life: not first of all words, but a conduct of luminous purity. And, in any case, the whole of his life, including his celibacy, is an example for all believers.

---

12. Matt 19:21. When Paul speaks of the Christians of Corinth who lived in celibacy, he says, "Now concerning virgins, I have no command of the Lord" (1 Cor 7:25). It has been observed that if Paul knew the saying of Matt 19:12, he did not see a "command of the Lord" in it (O. Kuss, *Das Neue Testament,* vol. 6 [Regensburg: Pustet, 1940] 148).

13. Strack-Billerbeck, 2:372-73.

14. Compare Matt 19:11 with 13:11.

## Jesus and Marriage

Daily life in Nazareth, bathed in Joseph's and Mary's love, constantly presented Jesus with the clearest example of love transfigured by grace. He spoke of marriage with divine simplicity, without any denigration of the flesh, without any emphasis on spiritual love. It is, he said, "what God has joined together,"[15] that is, the union of a man and woman in one flesh and one heart.

He intended to restore love to its original splendor, such as it was "at the beginning" when God created human beings "male and female." As for divorce allowed by Moses, it came, he said, from hard-heartedness.[16]

Since he fully espoused our humanity, and therefore our sexuality, he must have normally, like every man, thought about marriage. That some Rachel or Rebekah from Nazareth wished to marry him when he was in the splendor of his adolescence—for he was handsome; I cannot imagine him any other way—was absolutely normal. That he was intelligent and open-minded enough to notice it is self-evident. He also knew that one can look at a woman to desire her and commit adultery with her in his heart.[17]

A perfectly free man, Jesus liked weddings and was at ease in their convivial atmosphere.

The joyful wedding at Cana is familiar to us. When he called his disciples and then revealed his glory to them for the first time, instead of taking them off for a good retreat in a monastery—Qumran for instance—he took them to a wedding feast. And he changed the water in the stone jars into a wine of joy.[18] Since he was well-mannered, he surely congratulated the bride for her beauty, as propriety demanded; on this occasion, one could even indulge in the Middle Eastern tendency to hyperbole.[19] He liked fine garments. He would have admired those of a Judith or Esther: one must don a festive robe, he said, in order to share in the banquet of the reign.[20]

15. Matt 19:6.
16. Gen 1:27; Matt 19:4, 8.
17. Matt 5:28.
18. John 2:1-11.
19. See note 3, p. 140.
20. Matt 22:11-13.

The image of a wedding came spontaneously to his mind when he spoke of the heavenly reign. He used it
—in the parable of the servants who were waiting for their master to return from the wedding-feast (Luke 12:35-38),
—in the teaching on choosing the place of honor at a wedding-feast (Luke 14:7-11),
—in the parable of the discourteous guests who neglected to answer the invitation extended by the king for his son's wedding (Matt 22:1-10),
—in the parable of the "wise" and "foolish" bridesmaids (Matt 25:1-13).

In his childhood, Jesus was tenderly loved by his parents; in his adulthood, Jesus tenderly loved children. Like any sexually balanced man, he probably desired to have children. He loved them to the point of literally attracting them to himself. And children, who intuitively recognize those who love them, crowded around him. He loved them so much that his disciples judged he exaggerated on this point. Therefore, they imposed order around him. "[They] spoke sternly [*epetimēsan*]" to the mothers who brought their little ones. But Jesus, as Mark relates, became "indignant and said to them, 'Let the little children come to me; do not stop them.' "[21]

Luke specifies that people brought him "even infants" *(kai ta brephē).*[22] Mark notes that he took little children "in his arms, laid his hands on them, and blessed them."[23] Matthew and Luke, in their overriding care for what they thought was Jesus' dignity, could not bring themselves to record that Jesus embraced children. But it must have been a habit with Jesus, since Mark mentions it in another pericope.[24] Was he remembering his childhood years in Nazareth when Joseph and Mary embraced him?

He also wanted the reign of heaven to be like a reign of children, for only those who are childlike are able to enter the reign. And when he looked at them, he thought of their angels who continually see the face of the Father in heaven.[25]

21. Mark 10:14.
22. Luke 18:15.
23. Mark 10:16.
24. Mark 9:36.
25. Matt 18:3, 10.

**At the Heart of Jesus' Celibacy**

*Intimacy with the Father*

The word "it is not good that the man should be alone" remains eternally true. And it is valid for all men, therefore also for Jesus. Faced with this word, Jesus said,

> I am not alone because the Father is with me.[26]

This word, pronounced during the discourse before the passion, closely resembles the word that stamps his adolescence when, at the age of twelve, he said, "I must be in my Father's house."

Never alone, always with the Father! At the heart of Jesus' celibacy and chastity is his intimacy with the Father. This intimacy was not like a circle within which he could have entrenched himself to be sheltered from other loves threatening to take hold of him, but rather it was an intimacy into which he drew all other loves—the love of Martha and Mary, the loving ministry of women, the repentance of the woman taken in adultery, the tenderness of the sinner who anointed his feet—and purified them in the fire of his holiness. He did not need to speak of chastity or propose it as an example because it emanated from his person, because it was identical to his vocation, because it was the reflection of his fundamental relationship with his Father.

*The Mystery of Vocation*

Like every vocation, this celibacy remains a mystery. The word "let anyone accept this who can" applies to Jesus' celibacy itself. Indeed, marriage is no obstacle to entering into God's intimacy. Much to the contrary. It is in procreation that a man and woman are most intimately associated with God's plan and complete the act of creation by giving birth to a child called to live eternally in heaven. At the same time, all human beings, whatever their state—married, celibate, or widowed—are called to love God with their whole heart, with their whole soul, with their whole strength. They discharge this duty of love by fulfilling their vocations, that is, by following the paths God opens before them. For certain persons,

26. John 16:32.

this path is marriage. Thus, according to the tribal customs of his time, Abraham walked before God with Sarah, his wife, and also with Hagar, the servant, and Keturah, a wife of second rank,[27] living in the company of these women in the presence of the Most High. Abraham became the father of the people of the promise. On Sinai, Moses spoke with God "face to face, as one speaks to a friend," and then went back to converse with his wife Zipporah.[28] Isaiah saw the glory of God filling the Temple, foretold the coming of Immanuel, all the while living with the woman who was called "the prophetess."[29] For other believers, the path is celibacy. Such was the vocation of Jeremiah, the prophet of the new covenant. God expressly ordered him to live alone, wifeless and childless.[30] Lastly, for others, the path is widowhood. Thus, Ezekiel, the herald of personal religion, received the call to live as a widower when his wife, "the delight of [his] eyes," died suddenly in his presence.[31]

For Jesus, this path was celibacy. Such was the vocation he received from the Father. A man completely comfortable on the emotional level, he must have been naturally sensitive to the love of women and children. There is no reason to think that his vocation—and the salvation of humankind—could not have been fulfilled in another way, that is, without the scandal and horror of the cross. His celibacy remains a mystery, as does his cross. His celibacy is part of the litany of all the sacrifices placed under the divine *it is necessary*[32] and which reveal the Father's will.

## The Symbolic Meaning of Jesus' Celibacy

Prophets' lives often involved symbolic elements which were teachings on a par with their oracles. The solitude of Jeremiah, the celibate, prefigured "the disaster" which was Israel's abandonment of God's Law.[33] The death of Ezekiel's wife foretold the distress of

27. Gen 25:1-6. Let us recall the case of Jacob and his wives Leah and Rachel (Gen 29:15-30) and of their servants Bilhah and Zilpah (Gen 30:1-13). According to biblical traditions, these people were the origin of the twelve tribes of Israel.

28. Exod 2:16-22; 33:11.

29. Isa 8:3.

30. Jer 16:2.

31. Ezek 24:16.

32. See pp. 115–117 above.

33. Jer 26:13; 32:42.

the Babylonian captivity.[34] What was the meaning of Jesus' celibacy? Several interpretations can be proposed.

Jesus' celibacy inaugurated messianic times. The reign of God is at hand. It is the hour of extreme sacrifices which allow one to enter the reign. The excuse, "I have just been married, and therefore I cannot come,"[35] is no longer valid when the Messiah stands at the door and extends an invitation to the banquet of the reign. We must be ready to leave everything, "house or *wife* [or *husband*] or brothers or parents or children,"[36] at the Lord's call. It was normal that Jesus, who demanded these extreme renunciations, be the first to give an example of them.

Celibacy is also a prophecy of the eschatological reign. A day will come, said Jesus, when "those who are considered worthy of a place in that age and in the resurrection from the dead neither marry nor are given in marriage . . . being children of the Resurrection."[37] Whoever lives in celibacy in imitation of Jesus states that he or she in some way anticipates on earth the life of heaven.

The Father revealed God's love in Jesus' countenance. His celibacy was one of the features of this face of love. Tradition likes to declare that Jesus is the spouse of the messianic community.[38] He was not attached to the love of one woman since he was to express the love that God lavishes on the whole community, a love which is similar to that of a man for his wife. In Jesus, the Father gave to the community of the covenant the spouse whom God had promised when God had said,

> You shall be called My Delight Is in Her,
>     and your land Married;
> for the LORD delights in you,
>     and your land shall be married.[39]

Let us finally add this: it is important to revitalize the value of these signs. They have meaning especially for those to whom God

34. Ezek 24:24-27.
35. Luke 14:20.
36. Luke 18:29.
37. Luke 20:35-36.
38. This title is based on Mark 2:19-20, Matt 9:15, and Luke 5:34, where Jesus is compared to a bridegroom and his disciples to the bridegroom's companions. The saying as it appears in the Synoptics expresses the faith of the community in the Risen Christ rather than a word of Jesus himself.
39. Isa 62:4.

gives the grace to understand them. Other signs equally meaningful could have been given.

## "I Always Do What Is Pleasing to Him"

How did Mary and Joseph accept Jesus' celibacy? How did they live it?

Let us rephrase the question: What father does not hope to see his children's children, which, according to Psalm 128:6, is the blessing par excellence bestowed on those who walk in God's ways? And what mother does not desire to rock on her knee her children's children?

When God granted to Elizabeth the grace of becoming John's mother, she declared, "This is what the Lord has done for me when he looked favorably on me and took away the disgrace I have endured among my people."[40] Now Elizabeth was Mary's relative *(suggenis)*.[41] The two women were intimate friends since Mary assisted Elizabeth during the last three months of her pregnancy. Elizabeth's words on the shame of being childless reflect well the environment in which Mary lived. Jewish tradition, according to Rabbi Eliezer (ca. 90 c.e.), dared to state, "The one who does not beget any children is like the one who spills blood." It was also said, "The one who has no wife is not a man."[42]

Once again, how difficult it is to enter into the mystery of Joseph and Mary! And how are we to follow Jesus' spiritual development? We can simply think that like all parents who love their children, Joseph and Mary completely respected Jesus' freedom and decisions. For it became obvious, especially after the incident in the Temple, that Jesus' way was mysterious and that it was set down by the Father's will. The rule of Scripture, applying to all, certainly was "it is not good that the man should be alone." But he, Jesus, precisely was never alone: "I am not alone because the Father is with me."[43] He spoke this word of unconditional love, "I always do what is pleasing to him."[44] He lived in celibacy because such was the will

---

40. Luke 1:25.
41. Luke 1:36. We do not know the degree of kinship between the two women.
42. Strack-Billerbeck, 2:373.
43. John 16:32.
44. John 8:29.

of the Father, because he always did what was pleasing to the Father. And he lived without children so that all human beings could become his brothers and sisters because such was the will of the Father. He could present himself before God's throne, saying, "Here am I and the children whom God has given me."[45] His celibacy is not solitude, but rather the house into which all human beings are invited to gather for the eternal celebration of the Father's love.

To the word of obedience which was at the heart of Jesus' vocation, "I always do what is pleasing to him," corresponds the word of obedience which was at the heart of Mary's vocation, "let it be with me according to your word." Mother and son resembled each other in the obedience of love.

---

45. Heb 2:13.

# Chapter 6

# Klasmata

After the miracle of the multiplication of the loaves, Jesus asked his disciples to gather the fragments *(klasmata)* left over "so that nothing may be lost."[1] Likewise, we collect here *klasmata* on two topics of interest to readers of the Gospels.

## THE UNLIKELIHOOD OF THE PARABLES AND THE TRUTH OF THE GOSPEL

As a master of hyperbole, according to the trait he had inherited from his mother,[2] Jesus sometimes pushed his parables to the point of improbability. "His parables are more akin to riddles to be deciphered than to comparisons. It is obvious that he often transforms daily facts into unlikely stories."[3] This unlikelihood of the parables allows us to guess at the unlikelihood of God's conduct: God's love is such that it is beyond our comprehension. If we put them back into the context of everyday reality, the parables make no sense. Put back into the context of gospel truth, they are sublime.

Here is a shepherd who loses one of his sheep. He abandons the ninety-nine others in the desert to go after the lost animal. What

1. John 6:12.
2. See pp. 58–60 above.
3. F. Brossier, "Les paraboles de Galilée ou la subversion du quotidien," *Le Monde de la Bible* 72 (1991) 26. With the exception of the parable of the prodigal son, the examples given here are quoted by Brossier.

imprudence! Having found the one, he is now faced with running after the ninety-nine which are scattered all over creation. And he brings back the lost sheep on his shoulders. What Galilean shepherd would behave in this way? But the God of Jesus, the heavenly Shepherd, indeed sets out to seek the sinner who has strayed and brings that one back to the community.[4] As for the ninety-nine sheep left alone in the desert, no need to worry about them: they have not budged; they are parable sheep.

Here is a son who leaves the family home, goes far away, squanders his inheritance together with his religion in dissolute living. When he returns home famished, in his tattered swineherd's rags, his father sees him from afar, runs to meet him, and smothers him with kisses.[5] What father would spend his time watching for his prodigal son's return? But this is how the heavenly Father, the God of Jesus, welcomes the sinner who comes home, and even organizes a feast to celebrate the sinner's return.

What peasant would be doltish enough to throw his seed on the edge of the path, or into stony ground, or else into briars? Pretty unlikely! But, if the seed is the word, if the sower is Jesus, if the field is the human heart, then it is possible that the seed might be received in thankless soil. It can also be received "in an honest and good heart"[6] and yield fruit a hundredfold.

The parable of the wicked tenants is also unlikely. The landowner of a vineyard sends his servants to collect his portion of the harvest from the tenants to whom he has rented the vineyard. Instead of treating the servants fairly, they beat them up, stone them, kill them. What is the master's reaction? He continues to send other servants. And the tenants continue to kill them. What should the landowner have done? Send the police? Instead, he sends his son.[7] What master would act in this manner? But this is what the God of Jesus had done. God had sent the prophets; then God sent God's own Son.

A master comes back from a wedding banquet. His servants have been waiting, "dressed for action" and with "lamps lit." What is he going to do? Instead of saying, "Good night. Let's go to bed,"

4. Luke 15:3-7.
5. Luke 15:20 *(katephilēsen)*.
6. Luke 8:15.
7. Matt 21:33-46; Mark 12:1-12; Luke 20:9-19.

he tells them, 'Sit down at the table; I'm going to serve you." Surely an unlikely thing. But this was precisely what Jesus did. And the conclusion of the first half of the parable is in the form of a beatitude, "Blessed are those slaves whom the master finds alert when he comes."[8]

The parable of the ten bridesmaids takes first prize in this festival of unlikelihood. Everything is exaggerated. But what a jewel! Here are the ten bridesmaids who are supposed to enliven the wedding with their gracefulness, their songs, and their dances and who are sleeping away like ordinary maids. What a fine wedding! The bridegroom arrives late. In the Near East, a good delay is part of the feast. But it is not the bridegroom who should arrive late; it is the bride since it is she who is led from her parents' home to her husband's. Anyhow, at midnight, everybody wakes up. The improvident bridesmaids, who did not have enough oil for their lamps, run in haste to the store. At midnight? Naturally, the merchants— who are parable merchants, therefore always in readiness when and where needed—are waiting for them behind the counter. In the meantime, the cortege, which had tarried so long, sets out at a brisk pace. The negligent bridesmaids do not succeed in catching up with it. People quickly throng into the wedding hall, and the door is shut. The bridegroom, who has as his sole duty attending to the bride, takes on the role of gatekeeper and checks on those who enter. When the latecomers at last arrive, he claims not to know them. How is this? Does not he know the bridesmaids? Besides, they could have retorted, "And who was late in the first place?" Everything in this parable is unbelievable. But the essential point is strongly affirmed, "Keep awake therefore, for you know neither the day nor the hour."[9]

The unlikely details in the parables often aim first at catching the listeners' attention. Certain "embellishments"[10] in the parables are so colorful that no one can forget them. No one is fooled either. And Jesus supposed that his listeners had some common sense and knew how to interpret, relativize, and understand.

Beyond the improbable details, Jesus asserted, with sovereign authority, the absolute demands of God and the gospel. How can

8. Luke 12:36-38.

9. Matt 25:13.

10. *Ausschmückungen*, according to J. Jeremias, *Die Gleichnisse Jesu*, 4th ed. (Göttingen: Vandenhoek & Ruprecht, 1956) 20.

we forget that a debtor who owes his master ten thousand talents, that is, the fantastic sum of some twelve million dollars, is obviously unable to reimburse him? That, indeed, this is our sinful condition before God? That we must forgive seventy times seven times, that is, without counting? That we must cut off our hand and pluck out our eye rather than let ourselves fall into occasions of sin?[11] The unlikely stories of the parables attest that the service of God is an absolute.

We have seen the same absolute in Mary's Magnificat. Mary's absolute is truly Jesus'. The principle is once more verified: like mother, like son. Like Mary, like Jesus.

---

11. Matt 18:21-22; Luke 17:4. Matt 5:29-30; 18:9; Mark 9:43, 47.

## THE "BROTHERS" AND "SISTERS" OF JESUS

Matthew's and Luke's traditions, which seem to be independent from one another, attest the virginal conception of Jesus. But they do not tell us how Joseph and Mary lived their marriage afterwards. People "thought," Luke writes,[1] that Jesus was Joseph's son. Therefore, it can be assumed that Joseph and Mary lived their marriage like an ordinary couple. The primitive community had no qualms about speaking of the persons whom the Synoptics, the Acts of the Apostles, Paul, and John's Gospel call the "brothers" and "sisters" of Jesus.

*The Synoptics* speak of them for the first time in the saying on spiritual kinship with Jesus. According to Mark 3:32-35 and Matthew 12:46-50, the mother of Jesus, his brothers, and his sisters were trying to see him. Jesus then declared that those who did the will of God were his brothers and sisters and mother. The parallel passage in Luke, 8:19-21, also mentions Jesus' mother and brothers, but not his sisters.

The Synoptics speak a second time of Jesus' brothers and sisters on the occasion of Jesus' visit to Nazareth, according to Mark 6:1-6 and Matthew 13:54-58. Luke 4:16-22 knows this story, but omits the mention of Jesus' brothers and sisters. On the other hand, Mark and Matthew even give the names of Jesus' brothers, "James and Joses [or Joseph] and Judas and Simon." We do not know the sisters' names.

The *Acts of the Apostles* 1:14 speaks of Jesus' brothers when it describes those praying with the Eleven after the ascension: "All these were constantly devoting themselves to prayer, together with certain women, including Mary, the mother of Jesus, as well as his brothers."

In his Letter to the Galatians 1:19, *Paul* speaks of "James the Lord's brother." This James must be the one who is named in the Synoptics at the time of the visit to Nazareth.

*John's tradition* twice mentions Jesus' brothers. First, in 2:12, when it records that Jesus went down to Capernaum with his mother and brothers. Second, in 7:3, 5, 10, on the occasion of Jesus' pilgrimage to Jerusalem for the Festival of Booths. The Gospel adds

---

1. Luke 3:23.

at this point, "For not even his brothers believed in him" (7:5). John's tradition concurs with the theme of opposition to Jesus by some members of his family, opposition that is recorded by the Synoptics at the visit to Nazareth. Acts, quoted above, shows that this opposition seems to have subsided (at least partly) after the Resurrection.

We may think that by speaking so freely of Jesus' family, the primitive community intended to insist on the humanity of the risen Christ. He had brothers and sisters.[2] But obviously, it was not concerned about specifying the exact degree of kinship of these "brothers" and "sisters." It may be that this degree of kinship was perfectly well known in the primitive community. Furthermore, the question of Mary's perpetual virginity does not appear to have been a theological preoccupation of the apostolic age.

Neither was it a concern for the most ancient ecclesiastical tradition. This tradition, represented by the prestigious names of Justin (d. ca. 165), Irenaeus (d. ca. 202), Clement of Alexandria (d. before 215), left no testimony on the subject.

Exegesis, working on texts nineteen centuries old and within an environment completely different from that of the primitive community, cannot succeed in reaching with certitude any conclusion on the true degree of kinship of these "brothers" and "sisters."

The most obvious interpretation would be that these are indeed children born of the marriage of Joseph and Mary. This is what Tertullian (d. ca. 220) thought, and, later on, Helvidius (fourth century).[3] Even if their testimony is not normative for tradition, we can affirm that other births after Jesus' would have in no way tarnished Mary's holiness. Rather, they would have been new blessings for Mary. Scholem Asch aptly summarizes the sensibility of Jewish piety when he writes, "Miryam became pregnant again (a third time). . . . Miryam's fame constantly grew and, in the town, people said that she had received the Lord's blessing and was des-

---

2. L. Oberlinner (quoted in Pesch, *Das Markusevangelium*, 1:324) declares, "The certitude [*Bewusstsein*] that Jesus was fully human is also shown by the existence of brothers according to the flesh."

3. Tertullian, *De monogamia* VIII:2, Sources chrétiennes 343 (Paris: Cerf, 1988) 164, and *De Virginibus velandis* VI. These two treatises belong to the period in which he had gone over to the Montanist heresy, therefore after 207. As for Helvidius, he is known to us through Jerome who fought his positions in his *De perpetua virginitate B. Mariae adversus Helvidium.*

tined to establish several houses in Israel. . . . Indeed, for the Jews, what was sacred was motherhood, and not a sterile purity."[4]

However, there is an objection to this interpretation, and it seems almost insurmountable. It comes from John's tradition. At the moment of dying on the cross, Jesus said to his mother, "Woman, here is your son." Afterwards, he said to the disciple whom he loved, "Here is your mother." "And from that hour the disciple took her into his own house." Even if we recognize the weighty symbolic value of the episode, it seems difficult to deny its historical reality.[5] Now, if Mary had had, besides Jesus, other children who could have taken care of her, it seems unlikely that Jesus would have entrusted his mother to someone whose kinship with her is not attested by a single text.[6] This appears even more unlikely because, according to Acts 1:12-14, after the ascension these "brothers" gathered in the "room upstairs" to pray in common with the Eleven and Mary while waiting for the Spirit of the first Pentecost. If these "brothers" had been children of her marriage with Joseph, how could Mary have accepted to go and live with a stranger? This presupposes that she would have had a large family of at least seven children—besides Jesus, four "brothers" and "sisters" (at least two); that she would have lived with them from ascension to Pentecost; that she then would have left her family in order to reside in a stranger's house. Is it reasonable to suppose all this?

It so happens that another interpretation of the title *brother* is possible. It does not have to beg acceptance from exegetes because it is in perfect accord with biblical vocabulary. Indeed, the Aramaic *aha* and the Hebrew *ah*, which mean "brother" and which the Greek

---

4. Sholem Asch, *Marie mère de Jésus* (Liège: Calmann-Lévy, 1958) 215.

5. John 19:26-27. R. Bultmann, *Das Evangelium des Johannes* (Göttingen: Vandenhoeck & Ruprecht, 1962) 521, denies the historicity of the scene because of its symbolism and its absence from the Synoptics. But this does not constitute a proof. The disciple whom Jesus loved says his testimony is authentic (John 19:15) and one cannot reject this testimony out of hand. Even if this testimony has been added to the primitive Johannine text in a later redaction, "that addition is not necessarily unhistorical," according to R. E. Brown, *The Gospel according to John*, Anchor Bible (Garden City, N.Y.: Doubleday, 1970) 922. And according to M.-E. Boismard and A. Lamouille, *L'Evangile de Jean* (Paris: Cerf, 1977) 442, "it seems certain that . . . the people are real, but *also* retain a symbolic character."

6. Origen notes, moreover, that "Jesus said to his mother, 'here is your son' and not 'here is this one who is also your son' " (*Commentaire sur Jean* I:23, Sources chrétiennes 120 [Paris: Cerf, 1966] 70).

*adelphos* translates, can designate not only a blood brother but also a cousin or nephew or, in a general way, any more or less close relative. Thus, Lot is said to be Abraham's brother, whereas, in point of fact, he is his nephew. Jacob is said to be Laban's brother, whereas Laban is his uncle.[7] The same ambiguity is found in the use of the word "sister." Thus, Tobias marries Sarah, the daughter of Raguel, his father's cousin and calls her his sister. On this point, some have spoken of "a vague Semitic 'tribal' terminology"[8] in use in biblical milieux. The brothers and sisters the Nazareth folks spoke of—in Aramaic—would then have simply been members of Jesus' family, either on Joseph's side or Mary's. The most common opinion is that these people were cousins.[9]

This interpretation is supported by the following considerations. Several women from Galilee, who had accompanied and served Jesus, stood by the cross with Mary, his mother. Among them, Mark and Matthew name a certain Mary, mother of James and Joses.[10] Now, James and Joses are placed among Jesus' brothers in Nazareth. It is highly improbable—this is the least we can say—that when speaking of Mary, the Synoptics would have called her "mother of James and Joses." It is more probable that Mary, the mother of Jesus, was a close relative of Mary, the mother of James and Joses.

This interpretation seems the most plausible. However, it is not incontrovertible. For when the Old Testament writers speak of *brother* with the meaning of a more or less close relative, they are always careful to specify within the context the exact degree of kinship.[11] And in the New Testament, the writers, who spoke Greek and knew well the difference between *adelphos* ("brother") and *anepsios* ("cousin"), never apply the term *anepsios* to Jesus' brothers.[12] But we may suppose that on this point the primitive community

7. For "brother," see Gen 13:8; 14:16; 29:10; 29:15. For "sister," see Tob 7; 8:4.

8. R. E. Brown, *101 questions sur la Bible*, Lire la Bible 98 (Paris: Cerf, 1993) 143 (*Responses to 101 Questions on the Bible* [Mahwah, N.J.: Paulist Press, 1990]).

9. This interpretation is illustrated by Ps 69. It is abundantly quoted in the New Testament. The primitive community identified the person praying in the psalm with Christ Jesus. In John 2:17, this community quotes verse 10, "Zeal for your house will consume me." But it avoids quoting the preceding verse in which the psalmist speaks of his brothers who are, he says, "my mother's children."

10. Mark 15:40-41; Matt 27:55-56; Luke 23:49. It is possible that this Mary is "Mary the wife of Clopas," whom John 19:25 mentions among the women standing by the cross.

11. See J. Gilles, *Les "frères et soeurs" de Jésus* (Paris: Aubier, 1979).

12. In Col 4:10, Mark is said to be the "cousin" *(anepsios)* of Barnabas.

kept the Aramaic term "brother of Jesus" and out of veneration applied it to those it knew to be his close relatives.

To conclude, on the sole basis of biblical data, we cannot confirm with complete certainty that Jesus' *brothers* and *sisters* are real brothers and sisters born of Joseph's and Mary's marriage. Neither can we affirm the contrary. But the latter opinion seems more probable.

Christian tradition favored a loose interpretation of the title of "brother" and "sister." The first attestation of this comes from the Protevangelium of James.[13] This is an apocryphal work which, in its most ancient elements, dates back to the second half of the second century. According to this, Jesus' brothers and sisters were stepbrothers and -sisters born of a previous marriage of Joseph. Tradition did not keep this hypothesis, but simply preferred to see in these persons other close relatives. Origen knew the opinion of the Protevangelium, but did not adopt it. He preferred to open to the Christian community the perspective of Mary's perpetual virginity. In his commentary on Matthew's Gospel (ca. 249), he humbly proposes, "As for me, I think it is reasonable to see in Jesus the firstfruits of masculine chastity in celibacy, and in Mary, those of feminine chastity."[14] In his commentary on John's Gospel (ca. 231), he had already presented as "a sound opinion that Mary had no other son than Jesus."[15]

This sound opinion has led to faith in Mary's perpetual virginity. Mary is the *aei-parthenos* (the "ever-Virgin"). This term is attested with certitude for the first time in Epiphanius of Salamis,[16] at the beginning of the fourth century. Since the fourth century, this term has expressed well traditional Christian faith, that is, the faith of

13. Protevangelium of James 9:2; 17:1; 18:1; 19:13-14. On the date of the Protevangelium, see E. de Stryker, *La forme la plus ancienne du Protévangile de Jacques*, Studia Hagiographica 33 (Bruxelles: Société des Bollandistes, 1961) 418. The assertions of the Protevangelium are improbable, marrying young Mary to a man who was already the father of six children (four brothers of Jesus according to the Synoptics, plus the sisters, therefore at least two). Obviously, such a marriage arranged by God would have lacked plausibility. Later on, people preferred to think that the "brothers" and "sisters" of Jesus were cousins rather than stepsiblings.

14. Origen, *Commentaire sur l'Evavgile selon Matthieu* X:17, Sources chrétiennes 162 (Paris: Cerf, 1970) 217.

15. Origen, *Commentaire sur S. Jean* I:23, Sources chrétiennes 120 (Paris: Cerf, 1966) 70.

16. See Denzinger-Schönmetzer, n. 44.

the Catholic community, the faith of the Orthodox community, and also the faith of the first Protestant reformers (Luther, Zwingli, and Calvin).[17]

We must not underestimate the normative value of this community's faith, this community which around the fourth century elected to believe in Mary's virginity and, roughly at the same time, determined the canon of Scriptures, therefore determined which were the inspired books, the only ones which are the source of our faith.[18]

It seems "sound," according to Origen's word, to keep the faith of this community.

17. See R. E. Brown, et al., *Mary in the New Testament* (Philadelphia: Fortress Press-Paulist Press, 1978) 65, n. 116.

18. "It is only in the fourth century that the decisions of synods and the pastoral letters of bishops concerning the list of biblical writings become common. At first they are meant only for local communities; later they become a help to the unification of different ecclesiastical regions." H. von Campenhausen, *La formation de la Bible chrétienne* (Neuchâtel: Delachaux & Niestlé, 1971) 304. See also *Le Canon de l'Ancien Testament* (Genève: Labor et Fides, 1984).

# Conclusion

The post-paschal faith, illuminated by the mystery of the Resurrection, has honored Jesus with titles of majesty, such as God, Savior, Messiah, Lord, King, High Priest. The Old Testament and Jewish tradition were familiar with these titles, understood them within the context of their time, and granted to them only a limited value. Thus, for example, all the just persons of the Old Testament could be called sons or daughters of God. But the Resurrection of Jesus transfigured these titles by conferring upon them a divine fullness. Jesus is not simply son of God: he is the only Son of God. As Paul says, "[he] was declared to be Son of God with power according to the spirit of holiness by resurrection from the dead."[1] He is Savior, but not simply like the judges of old, who saved the people on certain occasions when they were in difficult circumstances: his resurrection established him Savior of all humans of all times. He is King, but not like the ancient kings of Israel, whose kingships knew both grandeur and misfortune: in his capacity as "first born from the dead,"[2] his kingship extends to all universes and ignores the limitations of time. He is High Priest, but not only for the duration of one ministry and only for Israel: he is "great High Priest" (*archiereus megas*) for eternity, the one who "passed through the heavens"[3] and who opens to all human beings the doors of eternity.

1. Rom 1:3-4. According to Brown, *Birth*, 494, "the christology of Jesus as Son of God was understood only on the basis of the resurrection."
2. Col 1:18.
3. Heb 4:14, 15; 6:20. J. Blank, "Jésus-Christ," *Dictionnaire de Théologie* (Paris: Cerf, 1988) 319, writes, "Today, we continue to regard all of the Christological titles as post-paschal creations of the community; it is certainly pertinent in the majority of cases."

Now, this path of glory, which ends with titles of divine majesty, began in humility, to be precise, in the womb of Mary of Nazareth.

All along this way, which went from the crib at Bethlehem to the light of Easter morning, the conversation with Joseph and Mary accompanied Jesus. Even in his public life, he kept in his mind the memory of Nazareth, as all human beings keep in their minds the memory of their childhood. It was within this conversation with Joseph and Mary that Jesus' personality was formed.

The love of a man and woman fashioned the face of the Son of God. The tenderness of Joseph and Mary was the environment in which Jesus' humanity developed.

# Bibliography

*Abbreviations*

| | |
|---|---|
| BJ | Bible de Jérusalem |
| CCD | Confraternity of Christian Doctrine (Bible) |
| Herders Kommentar | Herders Theologischer Kommentar zum Neuen Testament. Freiburg: Herder, 1964– |
| JB | Jerusalem Bible |
| KJV | King James Version |
| LXX | Septuagint |
| NAB | New American Bible |
| NEB | New English Bible |
| NJB | New Jerusalem Bible |
| NRSV | New Revised Standard Version |
| Safrai-Stern | S. Safrai and M. Stern, eds. *The Jewish People in the First Century.* 2 vols. Compendia rerum Iudaicarum ad Novum Testamentum. Sec. 1. Amsterdam: Van Gorcum, 1976. |
| Strack-Billerbeck | H. L. Strack and P. Billerbeck. *Kommentar zum Neuen Testament aus Talmud und Midrasch.* 6 vols. München: Beck, 1922–61. |
| Denzinger-Schönmetzer | H.J.D. Denzinger, *Enchiridion Symbolorum* 33rd ed. Rev. and ed. A. Schönmetzer. Freiburg: Herder, 1965. |
| *ThWNT* | G. Kittel, ed. *Theologisches Wörterbuch zum Neuen Testament.* 10 vols. Stuttgart: W. Kohlhammer, 1933–79. |

Abel, F.-M. *Géographie de la Palestine.* Vol. 1. Etudes Bibliques. Paris: Gabalda, 1967.

Aron, R. *Ainsi priait Jésus enfant.* Paris: Grasset, 1968.

Asch, Sholem. *Marie mère de Jésus.* Liège: Calmann-Lévy, 1958.

Aubert, J.-A. "Dichotomie sexuelle, antiféminisme et structures d'Eglise." *Le Supplément* 161 (1987) 53–62.

Benoit, P., and M.-E. Lamouille. *Synopse des quatre Evangiles.* Vol. 1. Paris: Cerf, 1965.

Blank, J. "Jésus-Christ." *Dictionnaire de Théologie.* Paris: Cerf. 1988.

Blass, F. *Grammatik des neutestamentlichen Griechisch.* Ed. A. Debrunner. 10th ed. Göttingen: Vandenhoeck & Ruprecht, 1959.

Boismard, M.-E. *Moïse ou Jésus.* Leuven: University Press, 1988.

Boismard, M.-E. *Synopse des quatre Evangiles.* Vol. 2. Paris: Cerf, 1972.

Boismard, M.-E., and A. Lamouille. *L'Evangile de Jean.* Paris: Cerf, 1977.

Boismard, M.-E., and A. Lamouille. *Synopse des quatre Evangiles.* Vol. 3. Paris: Cerf, 1977.

Bonnard, P.-E. *Le second-Isaïe.* Etudes bibliques. Paris: Gabalda, 1972.

Brossier, F. "Les paraboles de Galilée ou la subversion du quotidien," *Le Monde de la Bible* 72 (1991).

Brown, R. E. *The Birth of the Messiah.* Garden City, N.Y.: Doubleday, 1977.

Brown, R. E. *The Gospel according to John.* Anchor Bible. Garden City, N.Y.: Doubleday, 1970.

Brown, R. E., et al. *Mary in the New Testament.* Philadelphia: Fortress Press-Paulist Press, 1978.

Brown, R. E. *101 questions sur la Bible.* Lire la Bible 98. Paris: Cerf, 1993. (*Responses to 101 Questions on the Bible.* Mahwah, N.J.: Paulist Press, 1990.)

Bultmann, R. *Das Evangelium des Johannes.* Göttingen: Vandenhoeck and Ruprecht, 1962.

*Le Canon de l'Ancien Testament.* Genève: Labor et Fides, 1984.

Carmignac, J., and P. Guibert. *Les textes de Qumrân.* Vol. 1. Paris: Letouzey et Ané, 1961.

Carrez, M. *Les langues de la Bible.* Paris: Centurion, 1983.

Charlier, J.-P. *Jésus au milieu de son peuple.* Lire la Bible 78. Paris: Cerf, 1987.

Chouraqui, A. *La Bible traduite et présentée par A. Chouraqui.* Paris: Desclée de Brouwer, 1985.

Danby, H. *The Mishnah.* London: Oxford University Press, 1967.

Deiss, L. *Célébrer la Parole.* 7 vols. Paris: Levain, 1987–1991.

Deiss, L. *Marie, Fille de Sion.* Paris: Desclée de Brouwer, 1959. (*Mary, Daughter of Sion.* Trans. Barbara T. Blair. Collegeville, Minn.: The Liturgical Press, 1972.)

Deiss, L. *Printemps de la Liturgie*. Paris: Levain, 1979. (*Springtime of the Liturgy*. Trans. Matthew J. O'Connell. Collegeville, Minn.: The Liturgical Press, 1979.)

Deiss, L. *Synopse des quatre Evangiles*. Paris: Desclée de Brouwer, 1991.

Deiss, L. *Vivre la Parole en communauté*. Paris: Desclée de Brouwer, 1974.

Delebecque, E., trans. *Evangile de Luc*. Klincksieck, 1992.

De Vaux, R. *Les institutions de l'Ancien Testament*. 2 vols. Paris: Cerf, 1958–60.

*Dictionnaire de la Bible*. Vols. 1.1, 4.2. Paris: Letouzey et Ané, 1926, 1928.

*Dictionnaire de la Bible*. Vol. 6. Paris: Letouzey et Ané, 1960.

*Dictionnaire de la Bible, Supplément*. Vol. 6. Paris: Letouzey et Ané, 1960.

*Dictionnaire de Spiritualité*. 16 vols. Paris: Beauchesnes, 1932–1994.

*Dictionnaire de Théologie*. Paris: Cerf, 1988.

Dupont, J. *Etudes sur les Evangiles synoptiques*. Leuven: University Press, 1985.

Dupont, J. *Les Béatitudes*. 3 vols. Etudes Bibliques. Paris: Gabalda, 1969–73.

Eusebius of Caesarea. *Histoire Ecclésiastique*. Sources Chrétiennes 31. Paris: Cerf, 1952.

Fitzmeyer, J. A. "*Abba* and Jesus' Relation to God." *A cause de l'Evangile*. Lectio divina 123. Paris: Cerf, 1985, 15–38.

Gaechter, P. *Das Matthäus Evangelium*. Innsbrück: Tyrolia, 1964.

Gaechter, P. *Maria im Erdenleben*. Innsbrück: Tyrolia, 1953.

Gélin, A. *Les Pauvres de Yahvé*. Paris: Cerf, 1953.

George, A. *Etudes sur l'Evangile de Luc*. Sources Bibliques. Paris: Gabalda, 1978.

Gilles, J. *Les "frères et soeurs" de Jésus*. Paris: Aubier, 1979.

Gnilka, J. *Der Philipperbrief*. Herders Kommentar. 1968.

Grelot, P. *Introduction à la Bible: Le Nouveau Testament*. Vol. 6. Paris: Desclée, 1986.

Grelot, P. *Les poèmes du Serviteur*. Lectio divina 103. Paris: Cerf, 1981.

Gourgues, M. "Prier les Hymnes du Nouveau Testament." *Cahiers Evangile* 80. Paris: Cerf.

Guillet, J. "La chasteté de Jésus-Christ." *Les ambassadeurs du Christ*. Ed. P. Rolland. Lire la Bible 92. Paris: Cerf, 1991.

Hänggi, A., and I. Pahl. *Prex Eucharistica*. Fribourg: Ed. Universitaires, 1968.

*Hymnes et Prières de l'Egypte Ancienne*. Littératures anciennes du Proche-Orient. Paris: Cerf, 1980.

Ignatius of Antioch, *Lettre aux Ephésiens*. Sources Chrétiennes 10. Paris: Cerf, 1958.

Jaubert, A. *Approches de l'Evangile de Jean*. Parole de Dieu. Paris: Seuil, 1976.

Jeremias, J. *Die Gleichnisse Jesu*, 4th ed. Göttingen: Vandenhoek and Ruprecht, 1956.

Jeremias, J. *Jérusalem au temps de Jésus*. Paris: Cerf, 1967.

Jeremias, J. *Les paraboles de Jésus*. Paris: Mappus, 1962.

Jeremias, J. "La prière quotidienne dans la vie du Seigneur et dans l'Eglise primitive." *La Prière des Heures*. Lex Orandi 35. Paris: Cerf, 1963.

Jeremias, J. *Théologie du Nouveau Testament*. Lectio Divina 76. Paris: Cerf, 1973.

Josephus, Flavius. *De Bello Judaico*. Vol. 2:1. München: Kösel, 1963.

Justin Martyr. *Dialogue with Trypho the Jew*.

Kieffer, P., and L. Rydbeck. *Existence païenne au début du Christianisme*. Paris: Cerf, 1983.

Kraus, H.-J. *Psalmen*. Biblischer Kommentar Altes Testaments. Ed. Siegfried Hermann and Hans W. Wolff. Neukirchen: Neukirchener Verlag, 1960.

Kuss, O. *Das Neue Testament*, Vol. 6. Regensburg: Pustet, 1940.

Lagrange, M.-J. *Evangile selon Saint Luc*. Etudes Bibliques. Paris: Gabalda, 1927.

Lagrange, M.-J. *L'Evangile de Jésus-Christ*. Etudes Bibliques. Paris: Gabalda, 1928.

Laurentin, R. *Court Traité sur la Vierge Marie*, 5th ed. Paris: Lethielleux, 1967.

Laurentin, R. *Les Evangiles de l'enfance du Christ*. Paris: Desclée & Desclée de Brouwer, 1982.

Lauret, B. *Initiation à la Pratique de la Théologie Dogmatique*. Vol. 1. Paris: Cerf, 1982.

Le Déaut, R. *La nuit pascale*. Analecta Biblica 22. Rome: Biblical Institute Press, 1963.

Le Déaut, R. *Targum du Pentateuque*. 2 vols. Sources Chrétiennes 245, 256. Paris: Cerf, 1978–79.

Legrand, H. *A cause de l'Evangile*. Lectio Divina 123. Paris: Cerf, 1985.

Lentzen-Deis, F. *Die Taufe Jesu nach den Synoptikern*. Frankfurt am Main: J. Knecht, 1970.

Léon-Dufour, X. *Etudes d'Evangile*. Paris: Seuil, 1965.

*Letter of Aristeas*. Sources Chrétiennes 89. Paris: Cerf, 1962.

Livio, J.-B. "Les fouilles chez les religieuses de Nazareth." *Le Monde de la Bible* 16 (1988) 28–36.

Lohmeyer, E. *Das Evangelium des Matthäus*. Göttingen: Vandenhoeck and Ruprecht, 1958.

Maillot, A. *Marie, ma Soeur*. Paris: Letouzey et Ané, 1990.

Mora, V. *La symbolique de la création*. Lectio Divina 114. Paris: Cerf, 1981.

Mussies, G. "Greek in Palestine and the Diaspora." See Safrai-Stern.

Mussner, F. *Traité sur les Juifs.* Cogitatio fidei 109. Paris: Cerf, 1981.

Narchel, W. *Abba, Père.* Analecta Biblica 19. Rome: Biblical Institute Press, 1963.

Origen. *Commentaire sur l'Evangile selon Matthieu.* Sources chrétiennes 162. Paris: Cerf, 1970.

Origen. *Commentaire sur S. Jean.* Sources Chrétiennes 120. Paris: Cerf, 1966.

Perrot, Ch. *La lecture de la Bible dans la Synagogue.* Hildesheim: Gerstenberg, 1973.

Pesch, R. *Das Markusevangelium.* Herders Kommentar. Band 2, Teil 1. 1976.

Prabhu, G. M. Soares. *The Formula Quotations in the Infancy Narrative of Matthew.* Analecta Biblica 63. Rome: Biblical Institute Press, 1986.

Rabin, Ch. "Hebrew and Aramaic in the First Century." See Safrai-Stern.

Rahner, K. *Aimer Jésus.* Jésus et Jésus-Christ 24. Paris: Desclée de Brouwer, 1985.

Ratzinger, J. *Einführung in das Christentum,* 5th ed. München: Kosel, 1968.

Reicke, B., and L. Rost, eds. *Biblisch-historisches Wörterbuch.* Göttingen: Vandenhoeck and Ruprecht, 1962-.

Safrai-Stern. *The Jewish People in the First Century.* Vol. 2. Ed. S. Safrai and M. Stern, in cooperation with D. Flusser and W. C. Van Unnik. Van Gorcum, Assen/Amsterdam, 1976.

Schürmann, H. *Das Lukasevangelium.* Herders Kommentar. Band 3, Teil 1. 1969.

Schlatter, A. *Der Evangelist Matthäus.* Stuttgart: Calwer Verlag, 1957.

Schwab, M. *Le Talmud de Jérusalem.* Vol. 1. Paris: Maisonneuve, 1960.

Spicq, C. *Notes de Lexicographie Néo-Testamentaire.* Göttingen: Vandenhoeck & Ruprecht, 1978.

Spicq, C. *Notes de Lexicographie Néo-Testamentaire, Supplément.* Göttingen: Vandenhoeck & Ruprecht, 1982.

Strack, H. L., and G. Stemberger. *Introduction au Talmud et au Midrash.* Paris: Cerf, 1986.

Stryker, E. de. *La forme la plus ancienne du Protévangile de Jacques.* Studia Hagiographica 33. Bruxelles: Société des Bollandistes, 1961.

Tertullian, *De monogamia,* VIII:2. Sources Chrétiennes 343. Paris: Cerf, 1988.

Vermes, G. "Jesus the Jew." *Jesus' Jewishness.* Ed. J. H. Charlesworth. New York: The American Interfaith Institute-Crossroad, 1991.

Vermes, G. *Jésus le Juif.* Jésus et Jésus-Christ. Paris: Desclée de Brouwer, 1978.

von Campenhausen, H. *La formation de la Bible chrétienne.* Neuchâtel: Delachaux & Niestlé, 1971.